SOFT LANDINGS FOR HARD DAYS

life

SOFT LANDINGS *for* HARD DAYS

Wisdom, Companionship,
and Guidance to
Encourage Your Spirit

JOVIAN ZAYNE

PENGUIN LIFE

VIKING
An imprint of Penguin Random House LLC
1745 Broadway, New York, NY 10019
penguinrandomhouse.com

A Penguin Life Book

Designed by Cassandra Garruzzo Mueller

LIBRARY OF CONGRESS CONTROL NUMBER PERMALINK:
https://lccn.loc.gov/2026945561
ISBN 9780593994337 (hardcover)
ISBN 9780593994344 (ebook)

Printed in the United States of America
1st Printing

The authorized representative in the EU for product safety and compliance is
Penguin Random House Ireland, Morrison Chambers, 32 Nassau Street,
Dublin D02 YH68, Ireland, https://eu-contact.penguin.ie.

To the God who trusted me as a vessel,
thank you. The gift of being used by you
has eclipsed any feeling of sacrifice.

For my Jorgie: You will always be worthy
of the greenest grass, bluest skies, and softest landings.
Mama loves you to Jupiter and beyond.

Contents

PART II
Soft Landings for Hard Days

Author's Note

Though I am a certified coach, this book is not a substitute for one-on-one or even group coaching. Coaching is a personal and tailored practice bound by a specific code of ethics. Having the support of a licensed mental health professional, trained somatic healer, or certified coach is a responsible practice worthy of our time and consideration. As you explore options for your mental health journey, it is my sincere hope that this book will be a kind companion along the way.

The stories in this book are real, though for privacy, some details, including names, have been changed. Stories with accurate names have been shared with permission.

Introduction

I'm so glad you're here. Whether it was your desperation for soft landings, a curiosity or excitement, it's all pulled you toward relief, and brought you to the right place. That pull, that knowing, that's your gift. It reminds you that you're worth protecting, savoring, and loving. It tells you that you deserve to land more softly—especially on life's hardest days.

We live in a world that pushes us to be tough on ourselves. A world that rushes us out of the sweet and precious moments we're meant to savor. For too long, we have ignored signs of burnout and felt shame when we've come to the end of capacity. But within these pages, I want us to patiently unburden our spirits of the toxic expectations and dehumanizing rhetoric that have undermined our humanity. To treat ourselves the way we'd treat an innocent child worthy of our love: with patience, encouragement, kindness, and grace—and even a little playfulness. To let ourselves cry when we feel sad, remember we're worthy when we feel insecure, and rest when we're exhausted. This is what it means to give ourselves a soft landing.

Here, with me, I invite you to unwrap this timeless gift.

I PROMISE TO tell you lots of stories in this book, and I suppose there's no better place to begin than when I found myself in the hospital, wearing gray gauze socks, seven months pregnant with my first and only child.

I should start at the beginning. My pregnancy caught me by surprise. One month, I was horrified, bleeding through my white dress because my period had arrived early, and two months later, I was excited, staring at a stick with two blue lines, because it was eight days late. I stared at the positive pregnancy test that was about to change my life. Before going to tell my husband, George, the exciting news, I instinctively touched my stomach and whispered a promise: *To whoever was growing inside of me: I will love you and protect you.*

This promise meant I would form a cocoon, much like my womb, around my pregnancy—desiring to protect myself against negative inputs and stress. I was managing my affairs in the way we responsible ones tend to do. I wanted time to prepare and nest! My plan was to off-load my clients once I'd entered the third trimester. Even though I had a lot of responsibilities, I was keenly aware that I had, as a business owner, the privilege to enact boundaries that would keep my work stress to a minimum. I was prepared to give the right yes, or necessary no . . . or so I thought.

It was the final week of my second trimester, and I had just woken up from a delicious nap. I rolled over, turned on my phone, and instinctively opened my email. "OMG!!" I couldn't believe it, a wellness brand I'd been dying to work with wanted to partner with me. It was only two years prior that I had cut their logo out of a magazine and glued it to my vision board. All I could think was: *This is going to be a dream!* And for a few weeks it was, before it spiraled into an undeniable nightmare.

The nightmare wasn't sudden. There were red flags. The deliverables that kept changing without internal accountability, the meetings that would switch with no apology or consideration. The biggest flag: My liaison projected their insecurities onto others, especially me. I had a history of spotting this culture; wisely declining client opportunities that were values-misaligned. But this time, motivated by hidden fears disguised as a commitment to excellence, I said, "yes." As much as I was preparing to nest, I was also in "hustle mode," determined to make a strong impression before I began my parental leave. This determination clouded my judgment, weakened my boundaries, and made me hesitant to hold the client accountable. I cranked out work—not from a place of inspiration but from a place of fear and desperation. I was desperate to be relevant, and I was afraid to miss a "once-in-a-lifetime opportunity."

Turns out, some opportunities only need one time to hurt you.

Y'all, I remember one of my deliverables was to create and record a meditation practice. During the recording, I could hear the disconnect in my voice. I was unsettled and out of alignment. I was inviting people into a practice I wasn't ready to honor myself! I was rough on my body, working when I should have been napping. I was relentless, rewriting emails when I should have been eating. I performed like a machine, and in the process I disrespected my spirit and precious body. Instead of getting rest, I took impromptu meetings and engaged in stressful email exchanges. Instead of asking for help, I plowed through on my own. My self-talk sounded like, *It'll take too long to explain what I need, and by the time I do, I could have just done it myself.* Instead of prioritizing my health, I let fear make my to-do list.

In other words, I was confusing my desperation with my needs. I didn't need to be relevant, and I didn't need that opportunity. I needed to be my best for my pregnancy, and that meant that I *first* needed to be well. Being well meant honoring that season of my life—a season that asked me to prioritize my health and my pregnancy, not my job. (But let's be honest, is there ever a season that doesn't ask us to prioritize our health? After all, we are human *beings*, not human *doings*.)

Unsurprisingly, things came to a head during a routine doctor's visit. After taking my blood pressure, my doctor immediately sent me to the hospital. Can you believe even then I was still fighting to ignore calls from that client?! The client said they cared about my health, but their actions didn't show it. But more troubling was that *my* actions didn't show it.

Feeling afraid, I stared in the mirror of my hospital room. *How did I end up here?* I clutched my stomach and shook my head as tears filled my eyes. *I said I would love and protect you. I'm so sorry.* I felt like a failure. I was so disappointed in myself and too embarrassed to even call my parents. As George helped me back into bed, I finally determined to put my phone on do not disturb, pray, and let myself feel my feelings. George held me even closer that night, and in a way only he could, reached the depths of my spirit.

"Honey, you've done more than enough. We can walk away

from this work. Right now, I want you to be as nice to you as you would be to anyone else you love. It's time that you rest."

Later on, I called two of my closest friends, IJ and Brittany, and caught them up on everything. They each gave me the perfect amount of empathy and compassion—another soft landing I needed. Through their words I was reminded of my faith. A faith that says, in my weakness, God's strength is made perfect. My faith says I shouldn't let fear stop me from asking for the helpers or confidence that I need. My friends' words shattered my pride, and their empathy swaddled my anxious heart.

My hospital visit was my wake-up call. I'd been too lenient about the dysfunctional culture surrounding this client, and at the same time too hard on myself. While trying to be "excellent" at work, I didn't respect my body. And while trying to remain "relevant," I didn't respect my new season of life. Thankfully, I still had time to make new choices. I was alive, and my daughter would be, too. I ended the contract and didn't look back. To find my soft landing, I needed to recalibrate my priorities, pour into my spirit, and wrap myself in compassion. I needed to remember my precious humanity, and to protect it at all costs.

An Invitation to Land Softly

Throughout my life, I've needed millions of soft landings to get through my hard days. Hard days when a sudden illness would attack my body, when self-doubt stopped me from self-advocating, and when I refused to leave people who'd already left me. I've had days when I let a hater dim my light, felt shame for forgetting the cupcakes to my own child's birthday party, and thought, in a sea of content there's no way mine would make waves.

I know you've had tough days, too. Days when grief knocks you to your knees and days when the swirl of bad news feels like a fog you can't see through. And when these days come, it's so tempting to just keep pushing, work harder, or, on the other side, completely check out. In this, we often think we're disappointing everyone, including ourselves. This is when we tend to double down on ourselves instead of easing up.

We pull everything we can from our minds and bodies, then wonder why we're walking shells of who we used to be. As a human species, we've routinely overextracted goodness from the earth. And because we, too, come from the earth, we've also learned to overextract from ourselves.

It's not just the regular fifty-plus-hour workweeks that we excuse—it's also the packed weekends we schedule so we don't get "behind." It's the way we won't rest until our to-do list is complete, and the way we pressure ourselves into networking because we want to see what we can get out of each other. And then, when we don't follow up with the person we worked so hard to meet at that event (because we never *really* cared about meeting them), we feel bad about not building a relationship that we were never meant to have in the first place. We're exhausted from trying to prove we're still attractive, still worthy, still successful. We thought our generation redefined success through mass entrepreneurship and an illusion of work-life balance, but it's still killing us. Our to-do lists regularly outpace our capacity, and when they do, we tell people, "I'm sorry. I'm just so tired today." As if we haven't been tired for months. Years, even.

I'm going to say the thing we're all thinking: *The way we are living is painful.* Our casually accepted dehumanizing ways of being have collectively made our days much harder, and our need for countercultural soft landings undeniable.

This book is about how to create the soft landings—moments of gentleness, care, and affirmation—that will carry us through real life, the good and hard times. It's about building a practice of self-compassion and encouragement not just as a bonus, but as a prerequisite for living and loving ourselves more, especially on our hard days. Whether we're transitioning into a new career or navigating the emotions of caring for aging parents, we can all be transformed by the divine elixir of empathy, vulnerability, and encouragement—the perfect soft landing.

That's why, for us, landing softly looks first and foremost like remembering our humanity: expecting good effort, not perfection, and giving ourselves the space the world often doesn't to learn and evolve. Acknowledging and respecting our limits. Resting regularly, not just when we're exhausted. And feeling all our feelings, not just the ones that make others comfortable.

For a lot of us, this is hard to do, especially for Black Women. Life's hard days are exacerbated by institutional, structural, and systemic oppression, making the themes we'll be exploring in this book, like self-compassion and boundaries, resonate even more acutely for those of us who are and have been historically and legally minoritized. Yet, in a world that treats us so hard, it is *still* our birthright to experience soft landings in this lifetime and the next. **Our soft landings are our way back to love.**

Soft landings are a language and a mindset. Whether you're trying to find the courage to ask for an overdue raise or struggling to believe that it's not too late to begin again, we *all* need empathy and encouragement to survive the hard moments that are certain to come. This book is your invitation to step into this new way of living.

Manna from Heaven

This book was always inside of me, but it found its voice when the larger world slowed down and my intimate world sped up. A few days into 2020, my incredible daughter, Jorgie, was born. Our new family of three dutifully cocooned ourselves from anyone who hadn't had their flu shot, which meant we saw some family members, but not many. Before we knew it, what we thought was a temporary hibernation turned into nine months of necessary isolation due to the COVID-19 pandemic. We were on edge, disinfecting Chobani yogurt containers and wearing masks to vacant parks. I struggled with the reality that our parents lived thousands of miles away. I desperately wanted the physical presence of someone older and wiser to look me in the eye and tell me it was going to be okay. Sometimes, when Jorgie started crying, I would, too! I asked the same questions many new moms ask: *Is she eating enough? Will I ruin her if I watch TV while she's breastfeeding?* Meanwhile, I knew I'd be ruined if at the very least, I couldn't finish watching *Suits*.

As a new parent, my hard days where exacerbated when I didn't give myself enough grace to ease into my new reality. I would breastfeed in the nursery that was once my office, staring at the clock, which usually said something absurd like 2:14 a.m., and wonder, *When does this get easier?* Staring in the dark while Jorgie made new meaning of my breasts, I would muster strength from Psalm 23, "For thou art with me," and borrow courage from my tribe and more confident versions of myself (*You got this, Jovian!*). I would rock Jorgie to sleep until I heard my mother's voice echoing in my ears:

"Do your best, Jovian. Just do your best."

You know, there's a fine line between living up to your own standards and knowing when you need to reset them with self-compassion in mind. On the days I hadn't prioritized compassion, I landed harshly. The days I remembered me—remembered grace and my humanity—I experienced renewed peace and true joy. Those were the days I found myself landing softly.

Over time, the clarity for this book was crystallized during quiet moments in the nursery and during walks around my neighborhood. After one particularly long walk with Jorgie, I felt a spiritual urge to create something tangible for myself—something that would help me self-soothe during my difficult moments. I began to write myself more consistent and intentional notes of encouragement. I remembered my earlier visit to the hospital and wrote that pregnant Jovian a love note.

You don't have to have all the answers, Jovi. Put one foot in front of the other. Today it might be the left, tomorrow it might be the right. What small step can you take?

I've always journaled, but this was different. Sometimes these notes would come to me during a three-minute shower, or when I was feeding Jorgie and watching the NBA playoffs. These notes were insights, prayers, and lessons I'd learned over the years. When I was having a tough day, they were the words I whispered to myself. I'd hear myself say things like, *Jojo, put down the judgment and pick up the grace*. I labeled these notes "Divine Downloads to Land Softly," as much of it felt divinely inspired and provided. They were my manna from heaven and always seemed to come at the right time. For the day I couldn't wash another bottle, or the day comparison made me feel insecure, there they were—the words that helped me love myself even more. Before I knew it, I had a priceless collection of notes—the soft landings for my hard days.

The themes from my notes quickly surfaced and became the foundation for my five grounding invitations:

1) Be gentle with yourself
2) Feel your feelings
3) Believe you are worthy
4) Honor the seasons of your life
5) Appreciate life's goodness

When working with my clients, I've seen these principles applied as powerful mindsets, rituals, or practices. They have encouraged and guided thousands of leaders back to their humanity. Through these pages I hope they will guide you, too.

Dear Millennials

This book is meant to help all of us, across generations, live well, and, with God's help, I believe that it will. But I gotta tell you—most days while writing, I would look at my group chats and think, *Damn, I really hope I can finish this book. We* need *it.* And by *we*, I mean, my generation: the millennials. For us millennials, adulthood isn't what we expected. I say that loosely, knowing life doesn't owe us anything—though I'm sure we can all agree that the "work hard, save your money, and invest wisely" advice we were told hasn't safeguarded us from the world we're inheriting.

Across industries and sectors, we've seen massive global rollbacks to employee wellness benefits and engagements, many arriving in lockstep with the 2024 United States federal government's efforts to dismantle important equitable advancements. From new environmental hazards to declining health-care coverage, our ability to protect our humanity has gotten more difficult with trends of dehumanization happening at scale, all while our standards of "success" have gotten higher. Once criticized for being lazy and too unrealistic, as a generation we have lived through multiple recessions, a catastrophic global pandemic, war-filled civil unrest, and historic reversals to basic human rights. And on top of this, we're charged with cooling the boiling Earth!

Unlike any other generation, we also grew up with both an analog and digital experience, ensuring our adult development was accompanied by unique pressures, insights, and concerns. A significant portion of our lives is lived online, leading us to often have less meaningful in-person interactions. Our swipe culture has flattened the terrain of an authentic lived experience—the ups and the downs, the messy middles, the sudden confusion, and the incalculable heartbreak. In a quick thirty-second swipe, we can gloss over a friend's wedding, a declaration of war in a country we just visited while on vacation, and a peer's cancer diagnosis. And that's just on one social media platform. We are overwhelmed by our access to content and wrestle with what we can responsibly consume and cognitively and comprehensively process. We know there's a better way to handle technology, but we can't always find it. We are seemingly more connected than ever, and yet, in 2023, then United States Surgeon General Vivek Murthy declared that we are in an epidemic of loneliness, citing studies that reported that over 50 percent of adults are in some way lonely.

We've matured with the internet, and share stories on social media that aren't necessarily fake, but usually incomplete. We know many platforms are currently too flimsily and trained to be too culturally divisive to handle our tender truths. And so we limit what we share. Yet, because we've been trained to compare ourselves to others, we see each other's filtered existences and still use them to evaluate our successes. Navigating this minefield leads to many hard and nuanced experiences of psychological stress. And now, as parents, we are raising digital natives who will have even more nuanced and challenging relationships with technology and artificial intelligence.

This may be our new normal, but it's undeniably negatively affecting our mental and physical health. And it has only made it harder for us to live with authentic empathy, compassion, and encouragement—the core elements of any good soft landing.

Our elders and older cousins tell us of a different world, one that in many ways was safer, smaller, and more manageable. Families lived closer together, and unlike today, a village of support didn't have to be bought through an online agency. At the time I am writing this, we have officially become the sandwich generation—many of us are raising our own children while also providing eldercare to aging loved ones who live thousands of miles away. The sandwich era has always been traditionally tough, but as many economists and sociologists note, during this particular time in human history, it is especially challenging given cuts to government social programs, childcare deserts, rising individualism, and inflation (just to highlight a few reasons).

Every day, I talk to a friend who is struggling to manage this increasingly heavy load. We're identifying orthopedic surgeons for our mom's knee replacement while negotiating the terms of our FMLA with a passive-aggressive boss. But because we're so used to carrying it all—and carrying it well—when it all finally takes its toll, we question our strength, not the load.

We are harder on ourselves than we are on the systems and leaders that have betrayed us. For some of us, soft landings feel like signs of weakness, or like something we have to earn, instead of our divine right. It's why we can often talk ourselves out of a soft landing, like taking a mental health day or asking for help on a project.

Whew. Deep breath.

I know that might have been tough to read (honestly, it was tough to write). Though we both know, it's even tougher to experience. It's easy for us to feel shame or disappointment when we don't care for ourselves the way we know we should. But I hope all this illuminates that this isn't just an interpersonal problem. At the micro and macro levels, there are dehumanizing systems and policies rooted in capitalism and oppression that have become our personal practices and normalized routines. We need to go hard, not at ourselves, but at these dehumanizing systems; these are the things we need to reevaluate and dismantle.

This book is an invitation to hold ourselves precious in the midst of that slow, hard, macro-level change. It's a reminder that we can't wait for systemic overhauls to believe we're worthy of soft landings. We must live into them now.

If we're going to land softly, we have to notice and name our dehumanization so we can stop internalizing blame or isolating ourselves in our experiences. We are not alone in this! I believe, especially as millennials, we are primed to live out a generational purpose where we demonstrate the unlearning of dehumanizing behavior in real time. We can show future generations what it means to live more gently, empathetically, and communally. Our generational purpose is to help us all return home to ourselves while we can still recognize who we are.

This book is about how we can be more compassionate with ourselves in every way, shape, and form. We can reimagine our to-do lists. We can say enough to overproduction. We can rest. Every effort we make toward self-compassion is a breadcrumb that will lead us back to love.

Our soft landings are our perpetual invitations to remember our humanity and encourage our spirits. When we lean into our soft landings, we give ourselves grace before judgment. We realize imperfect words shared in grief matter more than fearful silence. We celebrate our progress, especially the times we have to crawl to the finish line. We continue to be in awe of the moon's impact on the ocean and amazed when a baby takes their first steps. We don't talk ourselves out of opportunities we've worked hard to achieve, and we let ourselves experience our emotions instead of ignoring them. When we live into soft landings, we trust ourselves with ourselves because we remember to love ourselves.

How to Read This Book

You might have guessed by now, but I'm a PK. That is, a preacher's kid. Not once, but twice over. Both of my grandfathers were beloved pastors. I adored my grandfathers, and in the churches they built, I felt seen, heard, and respected—a trifecta unfortunately rare for many young Black girls. Perhaps unsurprisingly, I was hesitant to tell you I am a PK. One, because of the historically divisive nature of religion, and two, because I thought you'd write me off as a "church girl," a stereotype that I mostly side-eye. (Also, FYI, I occasionally cuss, so there's that.) But honoring your story means experiencing the discomfort of the truth. And here's what I've learned: You can't find a soft landing in self-abandonment.

My experience in the Black church has been seminal—informing my beliefs, sense of worthiness, and connection to hope—all things we'll discuss in this book. My faith has been my rock. If we were playing spades, I'd call it my big joker. It's been in relationship with God and my family where I've come to understand the soft landing power of unwavering love and companionship, the ethos of this book. To know you are loved is its own kind of soft landing. And to find a faith that not only grounds you but also lifts you is another. Through my family's love and my faith, I have experienced an overwhelming number of soft landings for my hard days. They spring from the knowledge that I'm tethered to love—treasured and held, never veering too far away from those who "get me" and a Creator that *knows* me. I think of this inherited love as a guide and companion. This feeling, one of never walking alone, has been the ultimate soft landing, and it's given me courage and clarity about my own calling to walk with others. It's why I want this book to feel like a companion to you.

In part one, you will find five invitations to land softly: Be gentle with yourself, feel your feelings, believe you are worthy, honor the seasons of your life, and appreciate life's goodness. Each of these invitations can stand on its own as a mantra or a mindset that calls you into higher self-awareness and self-regulation. The practices you'll find in each chapter are ancestral, and as much a guide as they are a gentle call to action. They are grounded in emotional intelligence and supported by psychological and neuroscientific research.

In part two, there are reflections that ease you into soft landings of encouragement and comfort for your hard days, like for the day your body betrays you, or for the day you're afraid to fall in love. These supporting reflections meet us in our intimate moments and invite us to breathe, affirm, and, yes, reflect. In some ways, what you will learn in this book might feel like skills you want to develop (self-advocacy, emotional intelligence), and in other ways, it will feel like heart-expanding words from a loved one. Because, yes, I do love you!

When I facilitate workshops, I often invite participants to tangibly engage with the work. I may say, "You're invited to journal your thoughts on page 3." Consider this entire book your invitation to pause, reflect, feel, and choose. Pace yourself, scribble notes, and highlight passages that speak to your heart.

You will also notice an invitation for breathwork infused throughout the book. Breathwork can shift your mood and help you self-regulate. I know at times it can feel indulgent or even impossible to do this, but please know you are worth the pause.

Please remember that you have time to do the thing that keeps you alive—you have time to breathe.

This book will always have time for you. And if you let it, this book will sit with you. Let the words and spaces for reflection feel like a hand that's holding your own. In reverence to its title, *Soft Landings for Hard Days* isn't meant to be a hard read, so take your time—and by all means, skip around if you'd like. On days when you can't reach your friends or find enough hope and connection, I pray you open this book. Give yourself time to ease into the chapters, choosing your own adventure based on where you need to land softly.

I've experienced how one act of individual obedience can lead to collective transformation. So in that spirit, if you're compelled by what you read, please share, and give someone else the gift of a soft landing. When a passage helps you land softly, take a picture and send it to a friend. If you're so moved, share it online. Be in community! Start a book club! We shift culture when we land softly together!

As I wrote chapters in coffee shops and parks, I'd see people who reminded me of the friends and versions of myself I was writing to:

Both the friend who feels isolated in their success—unsure why they don't feel comfortable sharing their good news—and the friend who can't find the courage to make a career change.

The friend who thinks their perfection will protect them and the friend too afraid to start over.

The friend who worries they will never have the family they want, and the friend who never wanted a family and just wants everyone else to be okay with that.

The friend who didn't expect life to end up like this.

The friend who doesn't think their idea is good enough to share.

The friend who is falling in love, and the friend who is falling out.

The friend tired of caring for everyone but themselves.

The friend who had to bury someone they love.

The friend in the middle of a health scare.

The friend headed toward a divorce.

The friend who is doing the best they can . . . taking this sometimes very hard life one day at a time.

This book is for all of us who are ready to land more softly.

At times, the reflections in this book will feel like a photo album from college: priceless. Other times, they will feel like lessons you knew all along but seemed to forget: reassuring. That's because this book beats with the heart of our experiences. The epiphanies discovered through gut-wrenching loss and profound triumphs. It carries stories from epic New York City brunches and endless group chats. It flows from the wisdom of our ancestors, families, mentors, and coaches. And it most certainly reflects the counsel of licensed therapists (shout out to my own—hey, Dr. A!). Most importantly to me, this book is divinely inspired and woven together with the love and wisdom of a Great Spirit far beyond my strength.

Hope's Soft Landing

The true power of hope has buoyed generations and gives us an antidote to our helplessness. As I wrote these pages and fresh tears would fall I held on to this kind of hope, a belief that I would make it to the finish line. And as hope would have it, Victoria, my local barista, would appear at just the right time, pat me on the back, and whisper, "Keep going, Jovian."

As hope led her to me, hope led me to you, so, let me tell you what I hope for now. I hope this book helps you feel refreshed! I hope it feels like the friend who believes in you, has space for your feelings, and offers you space to fall apart and heal again.

I hope you remember that you're not alone, that you're always worthy of the space you take up, and that you need grace to protect your humanity.

And very honestly, as you read, I pray you feel my heart. The heart of a friend who will celebrate your wins and grieve your losses. The heart of an imperfect woman who, like you, has had her heart broken and lost jobs, friends, and confidence. A woman who didn't want to let anyone down, so she stayed in a job she hated. The heart of a woman who has dealt with comparison, toxic scrolling, body shame, and frustration. A woman who often wants to get it right the first time but also knows she deserves grace in the process.

I am writing for every version of us.

The broken me.

The torn you.

The insecure me.

The unsure you.

The depleted me.

The exhausted you.

The fearful me.

The scared you.

The expectant me.

The excited you.

The worthy *us*.

I hope this book feels like a salve on an open wound. But most of all, I hope you remember that you are a gift to this earth and that you always—I mean *always*—deserve a soft landing.

I'll talk to you soon . . . and often.

Love,
Jovian

SOFT LANDINGS
FOR HARD DAYS

Part I

The Grounding Invitations

In the next five chapters, I offer us five distinct invitations to land softly: ways to remember and say yes to ourselves. Each invitation gives us an understanding of how we can approach life with more compassion, grace, and care. These invitations are the foundation of how we can better love ourselves and each other. When woven together, they are a quilt we can wrap ourselves in to stay warm and covered, especially during life's tough moments. These invitations remain available to us, always giving us the option to say "yes!" to our soft landings.

CHAPTER 1

Be Gentle with Yourself

You have your humanity, and you must not allow anything to reduce that.

MAYA ANGELOU

When we first became parents, George and I, bless our hearts, were the type of millennial parents that teetered on doing too much. Our daughter, Jorgie, had everything she needed and then some. She calmed with the infamous Baby Shusher and slept with the best sound machine. Mind you, as an '80s baby, I remember falling asleep anywhere, bathrooms and kitchen tables included. But George and I were doing what every generation hopes to do—giving our kid just a little bit more than we had.

We were as prepared as new parents could be, though I'm not sure you can truly prepare for the times your kids will embarrass you. Like when they fall out crying in the store. Or, if they are like a young Jorgie, when they pass gas in church and then kid-whisper, aka scream, "Mom, was that you?!" (They can be diabolical, even on a Sunday.) Loud noises aside, I've learned that just as much as kids will embarrass you, they will also surprise you—and oftentimes, in the best ways.

One day, George and I went to pick up a then almost three-year-old Jorgie from preschool and were met at the gate by her teacher. She wanted to discuss Jorgie's recent bout with "rough hands." Apparently, for a few days, Jorgie had been snatching her favorite classroom toy from a friend. Now, as any good child psychologist will tell you, this is completely normal behavior at this age—toddlers will use rough hands when things don't go their way. Even still, on the way home, George and I went into overdrive reminding Jorgie about the need to use "gentle hands." (Bless our little hearts.) What we quickly realized was that Jorgie already knew what to do.

A week after the rough hands incident at school, we went to my brother's house for a barbecue. We were excited because we were going to meet the newest member of our tribe, sweet baby Nori. Jorgie stared, taking inventory of the three-month-old. Before I could say anything, Jorgie squatted in front of Nori's detached car seat and began to sweetly rub her arms. I stared at them, amazed, my eyes welling with tears. Jorgie, sensing my awe and determining it was unnecessary, looked at me, like, "Duh, Mama—even I know you can't be rough with a baby."

Still, I reinforced, "I love seeing your gentle hands, Jorgie."

"Yes, Mommy, I use my gentle hands with little babies. They are so *pwecious*."

Why We All Need Gentle Hands

In that moment, so much became clear. It's clear we know how to be gentle with precious and delicate things. We use gentle hands to put jewels in silk bags for safekeeping. We use gentle and patient hands to help our elders walk. And we gently swaddle newborns in soft fabrics. But what's also clear is that once we become adults, we no longer believe that we are precious. We think we don't need the things we once depended on as babies.

Think about it. We don't always acknowledge when we need help or rest. We don't speak kindly to ourselves when we mess up. And we don't like to respect our limits. Somehow, we've forgotten that even now, at our big ages, we are still those precious babies who need gentle hands, especially from ourselves. We might not need someone to swaddle us before bed, but we still need a gentle hand that will give us back rubs when we're sad or cover us in a blanket when we're tired. And, perhaps even more than the physical act of gentle hands, we need the spirit of gentle hands to bring about a cultural shift and a collective soft landing.

Gentleness is foundational to the practice of landing softly. Our gentle hands are tender, patient, and compassionate. Our acts of gentleness are how we advocate for our humanity, how we remember that we were never meant to do life alone, and that we don't have to wait until we're at the end of ourselves to ask for help. When we feel like things are going too fast, gentleness lets us set our own pace. Without gentleness, we aren't able to honor the seasons of our lives or let ourselves feel our feelings. It's in our gentleness that we accept our failures, messy middles, and heartbreaks. Gentleness helps us understand that our capacity, though flexible, is still finite—and that's okay. On the days we've hit our limit, our gentle hands don't push us to do more. On our hard days, like the days we make big mistakes and when our best just isn't enough, we don't need judgment or guilt; we need consideration and grace—we need gentleness.

The Many Textures of Rough Hands

In today's world, we sometimes move so quickly we don't even notice when we're living in an answered prayer. We're outrunning our lives, constantly grinding and hustling for more; often forfeiting the time to relish our hard work. We berate ourselves for missing left turns and feel guilty when we haven't completed our never-ending to-do lists. These small but very real ways that we are hard on ourselves add up. But thankfully, so do our small acts of gentleness.

At our big ages, we've likely heard or said, "Don't be so hard on yourself." But for some of us, it's easier said than done—especially when the ways we're more rough than gentle are second nature.

Let's do a quick audit:

- Do you feel guilty for taking a sick day?
- Do you apologize for wanting a nap?
- Do you constantly compare other people's careers to your own?

- Do you shame yourself for not having learned certain skills earlier?
- Do you have a hard time resting when your to-do list is unfinished?
- Do you resent how you care for others at the expense of yourself?
- Do you beat yourself up when your body lets you down?

Did you answer "yes" more than you wanted to? If so, that's okay. I once did, too.

In my work as a coach, I often see the heaviness that comes with operating with rough hands. With their permission, I'd like to introduce you to my clients Jasmine and Sean. They're just like us, well-intentioned, hardworking people who care about their family, friends, and career. They carry the burdens of performance and excellence we often feel, and this frequently leads them to choose rough hands over gentle ones.

Jasmine hangs up the phone with her elderly mom with a sigh. She's tired of arguing. That was their third conversation about why her mom has to stop driving at night, but it seems like they're just going in circles.

Ugh, I'm failing at this! Why can't I convince her to stop driving? Jasmine thinks to herself.

She checks the clock. Only five minutes before her next meeting. She opens Uber Eats and orders a burger and fries. She looks at the uneaten salad in the corner of her desk.

"Welp," she whispers, "looks like I'm failing at eating healthy, too."

What she really wants is to escape to the bathroom for a quick reset, but she's going to be late. Instead of letting her colleagues know she needs a second, she grabs her laptop, stands up wearily, and heads to the conference room.

Two desks over, Sean looks at his swollen ankle and drops his head in disappointment. A quick game of basketball with his son and now he's been sidelined from so much. He pulls out his phone and opens a video from their game in the backyard. He smiles, good memories suddenly flooding his mind.

A calendar reminder pops up on his phone: Tony in town. *Oh shit!* he thinks. *Tony and his wife are staying with us next week. Lisa needs me to help prep the house. Ughh, I'm already behind on so much. I've missed the gym, I've got yard work to do, this presentation isn't done . . . and now I can barely walk.*

His shoulders slump; he's beginning to feel overwhelmed, the pressure to get it all done starting to weigh him down. He wants to call his wife for some encouragement. Just hearing Lisa's voice would give him reassurance. His thumb hovers over her name before he ultimately closes his phone.

She shouldn't have to cheer me up. She's got enough on her plate. I don't wanna be another problem for her. I've gotta handle this myself.

Sean takes a sharp inhale, his back tightening, and tosses his phone and his feelings to the corner of his desk. He quickly opens the tab to his unfinished presentation.

Jasmine and Sean are doing the best they can with what they have, but the moment it doesn't feel like it's enough, they choose to go harder instead of landing softly. Like many of us, they choose to hold their breath instead of releasing the pressure. And instead of affirming their hard choices, their critical self-talk cosplays as accountability.

Here's the thing: Many of us think that what's keeping everything together is our hard work, and the moment we let up, everything will fall apart. We're holding too much weight, but because we haven't yet collapsed, we think we're fine. We don't believe we're the perfect candidates for micro moments of grace, even though that's exactly what we need. What are the beliefs that are underneath the enormous weight we continue to carry? *If we're not doing enough, getting it all right, or being useful, we haven't earned grace. We have to earn our fun, keep it all together, and always deliver with excellence. Our rest needs to be justified and our imperfections need to be corrected.* These beliefs and many others translate into the things we say to ourselves—the negative self-talk and small acts of self-deprivation that become so normal, they don't seem harmful. But every day, they are the insidious acts of dehumanization that chip away at our precious humanity.

When we believe we have to earn grace, we will never believe we deserve a soft landing. But when we experience the soft landing of gentleness, we untangle our purpose from our productivity and instead wrap our purpose and identity in grace.

Let's replay these scenarios, this time with small acts of gentleness, and see how Jasmine and Sean can find soft landings for their hard days.

Jasmine hangs up the phone with her mom with a disappointed sigh. She feels the sense of failure creeping up her neck. She doesn't run from it but takes it as a sign to take a few calming breaths. After a cycle of deep breaths, she whispers to herself, *You did the best you could with what you had, and that is good enough in this moment. You're in a tough position. I love you for loving your mother. Now, go love yourself.* She checks the clock and thinks, *Oh good, Tanisha is probably still at lunch. I'll ask her to bring me some fries from the café.* She sends a quick text and then grabs her salad. She stands up a little weary, but unbroken, and heads to the conference room already determined to leave her work at the office. She knows she needs a mental break tonight and she's committed to taking it.

Two desks over, Sean looks at his swollen ankle and shakes his head. He takes a deep breath. A quick game of basketball with his son and now he's been sidelined from so much. He pulls out his phone and opens a video from their game in the backyard. He smiles in spite of himself, good memories suddenly flooding his mind.

A calendar reminder pops up on his phone: Tony in town. *Oh shit!* he thinks. *Tony and his wife are staying with us next week. Lisa needs me to help prep the house. Ughh, I'm already behind on so much. I've missed the gym, I've got yard work to do, this presentation isn't done . . . and now I can barely walk.*

His shoulders begin to slump; he's beginning to feel overwhelmed, and the pressure to get it all done is starting to weigh him down. He's tempted to ignore how he feels. But he takes a deep breath in and lets it out. He repeats. Each cycle gives him comfort and space to think more clearly. He wants his wife's reassurance. After a few minutes, he feels more resolved: *I need to be honest*. He texts his wife.

"Hey babe. I know you've got a lot on your plate right now. Just letting you know I'm feeling a bit overwhelmed myself, especially with this ankle sprain. I'm gonna ask Tony to help me with the yard work, what do you think? I know we have to prep the house for guests. I'll call you later. Love you."

Feeling a bit relieved now that he's shared how he feels, he closes his eyes and takes another deep breath before returning to his presentation.

Jasmine's hard day was made harder with an internalized guilt trip and unrealistic expectations as a "good" daughter. She landed softly with her own gentle reminder to care for herself while she's also caring for her mother—food choices included. Sean's relief was in his release, not resistance. Jasmine and Sean didn't need to push harder to land softly; they needed permission to pause, breathe, and treat themselves gently. They needed permission to unburden and to feel.

Why We Play Rough

Watching Jorgie with baby Nori reminded me that we haven't always been rough with ourselves. But gradually, with new social pressures and technological advancements, as a society, we've moved further away from that instinctive gentleness—that deep acknowledgment of our sacred humanity. This change has been slow, persistent, and *everywhere*. It's hard to inoculate ourselves against its infection. Now, the use of technology is so embedded in our lives that we sometimes act as if *we* are the technology. We treat our bodies like machines—always powered on, relentless, without a need for rest or play—in our pursuit of accumulating more things. More money, more land, more access. We would work ourselves into oblivion if it meant we would have more things.

And it's because we've bought into this lie sold to us by capitalism: More things equal more security and more unequivocal happiness. This lie feeds our fears and conditions us to play rough. The destruction that a Western-industrialized, hyper-individualist capitalist society has had on our mental and physical well-being can't be understated. Playing double Dutch with the desire to always "have it all" and the awareness that having it all is utter bullshit has left us mentally haggard and physically unwell.

When we believe that we're machines who must produce to have value, we substitute our grace-laced gentle hands with rough hands that will keep us working under any condition. But when we remember that we are precious human beings, we can treat ourselves with gentle hands that push back against that lie and give us the soft landings we not only deserve but also so desperately need.

When we're in the prime of our careers, it can be increasingly difficult to give ourselves this gentleness. This time is a beautiful nexus of wisdom, experience, and expectation. And gentleness can often feel at odds with what society says: Your prime earning years are the time to go hard—with everything. It is harder to be gentle with yourself when you're afraid that if you don't grind now, you won't be able to enjoy your later years.

Our fears can overpower our gentle hands, driving us to burnout. Whether it's a fear of failure, unworthiness, or our own feelings, our fears can stop us from loving ourselves with compassion. But where fear has us handcuffed, grace has the key. Grace to rest. Grace to evolve. Grace to be helped. Grace unlocks gentleness, and gentleness unlocks our soft landings. At a time in our lives when our personal expectations have never been higher, and our bandwidths and attention spans have never been lower, we need to be gentle with ourselves. We need the grace to land softly.

How We Land Softly

In many ways, our larger culture has reduced the power of gentleness to trivial things. Being gentle is often coupled with the trendy "soft life" proposition, which at best urges us to prioritize self-care, and at worst, encourages us to disengage from responsibilities and effort. And while its tenets are about taking care of yourself, what's most notable is the emphasis on luxury care: regular hair and nail salon appointments, luxury trips to "treat" oneself, specialty salt baths, and other niche self-care regimens that promise to deliver us into a "soft life."

Before you say, "Now, Jovian, I know you love a good spa!" *Obviously.* But when my money is funny and I can't afford the time or dollars for regular spa treatments, am I voted off Soft Life Island? Is gentleness no longer a possibility? Our society has commodified and complicated simple acts of self-care. For those of us responsible for so much and so many—children, businesses, side gigs, doctor's visits, clients, aging parents—we have a lot of questions. And so do those impacted by the trauma of poverty. Do we need money to be gentle? Where is the soft landing that we prayed for? Do we need new gadgets to be gentle?

Here's the good news: A return to *true* gentleness doesn't require any external resources. Unlike the quick fizzles of bath salts, true gentleness lasts as long as we commit to honoring our own humanity. This is why being gentle is so countercultural. The soft landing of gentleness isn't about performative or suggested self-care but about the discipline of self-compassion. It's about recognizing our needs and communicating them to ourselves, and then to others.

We all have needs. Gentleness helps us to see these needs as:

Rest: Our bodies and minds need enduring and restorative rest, not restless guilt-filled naps.
Grace in complications: Without shame or resistance, we need grace to evolve into who we are always becoming.
Permission to feel: Our mental, emotional, and physical health are all connected. We need permission to feel our truth in order to experience healthy lives and relationships.
Help: Instead of feeling the shame that comes from overpromising and underdelivering, we need safe places where we can get help and support.

Now look, I'm a preacher's kid, so of course I'm going to bring up Jesus. And whether you believe in him or not, I think he serves as a great example of the importance of honoring our needs. Because even Jesus, as said to be God in the flesh, needed, *in his flesh*, rest, help, grace to grow, and permission to feel his feelings. And, like many of us, he was questioned and persecuted when he prioritized these things. His righteous anger toward exploitative selling in the temple was met with indignance, and his decision to rest in the midst of a storm was baffling. But through it all, Jesus never stopped prioritizing the things that made him human, the things that required gentleness. The things that made him *like us*. He took extended breaks after performing miracles, and he cried when his friends abadoned him during his final hours in the garden of Gethsemane.

Whether it's professionally or in our personal relationships, we have the capacity to experience more soft landings by gently acknowledging and meeting our needs. When my mind needs a mental break, my decision to close my laptop can be a radical act of gentleness. When you need peace, but your group chats have become a breeding ground for anxiety, your gentle hands can put all of them on mute.

I know we can do this because I've seen the spirit of our gentle hands give the most heart-expanding soft landings. Our gentle hands schedule therapy sessions and cook homemade meals for sick friends. They put our phones on do not disturb and help us start new, life-giving hobbies. They squeeze clammy hands that need reassurance, and they dab our tears but don't demand that they stop flowing. When we're exhausted and lonely, our gentle hands feel like understanding advocates willing to protect the precious parts of us, the all of us. Our gentle hands give us what we need.

The Need for Rest

Rest is a practice and a divine right. A divine right because it's hardwired into our bodies as a basic physiological needs. It's something we must practice because we're living within social systems built on extracting the life out of us. We are daily dysregulated by capitalism's call to overconsume and overwork, making the need for rest paramount, though to truly experience it while dysregulated is hard to grasp.

There are enough clinical studies that help us know intellectually that we need rest. As Bessel van der Kolk explores in his book *The Body Keeps the Score*, every time we push ourselves beyond our limits, our bodies keep score. The stress we carry becomes more deeply embedded, and the risk for health challenges grows greater. Yet many of us still struggle to embrace this particular form of gentleness. Because of what we've seen at the macro and micro levels, from industry leaders who work on "vacation," to family members who take on too much, it is overwhelmingly countercultural to rest. But I think, for many of us, it's not that we're not capable of resting. To land softly, we might also need *new* permission to rest.

My dad and I have a standing date: Every year we attend the Executive Leadership Council's fall gala. The 2025 gala was no different. Plans were made and expectations were set. I was excited, but as the date neared, my body started to show signs of fatigue. No method of motivation seemed to be working: The promise of business development didn't move me, and the hope of a good party with friends didn't excite me. My body was *tired*. I knew it on every level, especially as a coach who sees this type of exhaustion in clients, but I still resisted saying the words *I can't go*. My last-ditch effort? I set a short timer (my go-to hack) and tried to pack. I circled a half-empty suitcase twenty times before throwing up my hands and falling back on my bed. Finally, I let myself imagine the possibility of not attending the gala. In seconds, imaginary weights lifted from my shoulders.

I called my parents, preparing to tell them the whole story—why I was so tired, why I might need to still go, etc. Thirty seconds in, my dad lovingly cut me off. In his no-nonsense way he said:

"Honey—you need to rest. That is the priority. Take care of yourself."

My mom, in her soothing voice, echoed those sentiments and reminded me that my decision to rest was a spiritual act of divine obedience. By the end of our call, I didn't even remember why I thought I had to attend the gala in the first place!

So often we need help doing the hard thing. And when there is a lot to be done, that hard thing is resting.

One day I asked George what's the best soft landing I've ever given him. Without hesitation he said, "You gave me permission to rest."

He went on.

"My dad never used an alarm clock and he used to tell me, 'Responsibility will wake you up.' I didn't understand that at first, but now I can't sleep well if I know I have things to do for our family—things to fix, people to support. But one day, when I was spiraling and really tired from everything . . . Jorgie, clients, project edits . . . you noticed and told me to go to bed. It was crazy because it was the middle of the day, but you didn't hesitate. You meant it. For the first time in a long time, I really slept."

My parents' permission helped me to rest. My permission helped George to rest.

I'd venture to guess that most of us are responsible people who rest better when our work is done. Yet, our real lives are messy: a bunch of loose ends and unfinished business. We need permission to sleep peacefully on that bed of loose ends and "coulda, woulda, shouldas." We can't always rely on other people to give us the permission we have to give ourselves. There will be days when George can't reach me, and I can't reach him or my parents. But when we need it, my prayer is that we'll still hear each other's voices.

What voice once gave you permission to rest? Can you still hear it? What does your voice of permission sound like? Borrow that voice until it becomes your own. If we want to have a soft landing, we must cultivate an internal voice of gentleness that compels us to rest and to take good care of ourselves. We can't do what we're uniquely meant to do on this earth if we're constantly depleted.

Our obedience to rest is connected to our commitment to purpose. Our divine calling requires us to rest. Our rest triggers our dreams, and our dreams are manifestations of the divine. Our dreams birth new realities that cure diseases, end wars, and create life-affirming art. Our rest also matters to each other. I see you better when I'm rested. You hear me more clearly when you've rested. Rest is a signal that we take each other, and our lives, seriously.

Our destiny is too important for the prideful denial of rest. The need for rest is primal; its impact on our bodies is irreplaceable. When we realize that our dreams deserve our full tank, we will refuse to run on fumes. The soft landing we want is on the other side of rest—rest we don't need to work any harder to deserve; rest that is divinely ours right now.

Don't let them tell you that you'll sleep when you're dead. You'll just be dead. So you might as well get that good nap now.

The Need for Grace in Complications

Children's books are such a gift. They illuminate life lessons we tend to forget as grown-ups. One of my favorites is *The Rabbit Listened* by Cori Doerrfeld. In this tenderly told and beautifully illustrated book, we follow the journey of Taylor, a child who builds an impressive tower of blocks only to have it torn down by a murder of crows. First, the chicken comes to Taylor to talk about the destroyed blocks. Taylor retreats. Then the bear stomps over in a rage inviting Taylor to scream with him. Taylor screams. All sorts of animal friends come to Taylor, all hoping to make them feel better, but they don't. But then the rabbit comes. The rabbit quietly sits with Taylor. Together they remain silent until Taylor says, "Please stay with me." And so, the rabbit does. The rabbit stays as Taylor locates their feelings and in time processes them—the sadness, rage, confusion. The rabbit embraces all of Taylor's parts: the angry, despondent, and silly. The rabbit's presence is a soft landing.

Our lives can be unexpectedly complicated. One day we're taking out the trash and the next we're in the middle of a messy divorce. We've got complicated feelings about our bodies, the state of the world, and our part in fixing it all. It's easy to think it should all be black and white, but we know better. We've lived in the gray long enough to know this gray—*this* is the real world. We are real people who represent a "both/and" and everything in between. The anger and the apathy. The joy and the sorrow.

Instead of trying to fix or explain every complication within or around us, sometimes the gentlest way to handle a complicated reality is to simply acknowledge it. To love all our parts. To be the rabbit with ourselves. Through this act of love comes our self-esteem and self-confidence. Sure, we may want to improve in one way or another, or fix things, but along the path of self-mastery, we can still gently love our "complications." Our light shines, not in spite of our inconsistencies but through them.

Our complicated days are made better with our grace, not our harsh judgment. For example, you're caring for a loved one with health challenges. There will be days when you have no answers, just exhaustion. It's okay to say, *This is hard and I feel like I can't win. I am tired and I want to do more, but today I've got nothing left*. Grace reminds us that it *is* disorienting to care for aging parents, and it *is* challenging to raise a child with autism without support. Grace can meet us in the mess. It holds us when we're grieving and supports us when we're secretly embarrassed by our success.

We contain multitudes. When we embrace the things that make us complicated, the kaleidoscope of feelings and realities that make up our days and nights, we can land more softly. There is a relief when we finally stop judging our truth and simply accept it for what it is. Compassion erupts in our acceptance. And only through this acceptance can we then attend to our truth—giving ourselves whatever help, support, and attention we need.

The Need to Feel Our Feelings

Some of us know what it's like to be called sensitive. That is, people who feel deeply. If you're into zodiac signs, you may say that people who have the Cancer sign are "feelings" type of people. But whether you're a Cancer, Aries, or a fellow Virgo (ha, your assumption was correct about me!), our feelings are so important to how we *all* bear witness to our experiences. As we'll talk about in chapter 2, our feelings don't always tell the whole story, but they do give us important information. They are how we connect with one another and how we better understand ourselves. Our emotions signal our needs and help us to make sense of what we're going through. To deny our feelings is to deny ourselves.

Most significantly, when we feel, we begin to power our empathy. When Marquita's sister died, a depth of empathy is what led our friend Horecee to call Marquita every day for six months. Knowing how it feels to finally get an overdue promotion is what led Jason to host a celebratory happy hour for Morgan. And when we've felt the power of transformative love in our own lives, we're honored to say yes to a cousin's wedding invitation. We're better people when we can feel each other's joy and carry each other's burdens.

Our feelings reflect our shared and sacred humanity. And it's in that shared humanity that we find our most resonant connections. When we see the humanity in each other, we help each other land more softly. But when we don't see it, we make our hard days even harder. When we feel our feelings, we can better administer love, and truly see each other. And that right there might be the softest landing we can get: the soft landing of being seen.

The Need for Help

For some of us, the real problem with asking for help is that we first have to admit that we need other people. This is difficult to admit when we've been fed the lie that doing it alone is more rewarding than doing it with others. But somewhere, an ancestor is gently whispering the African proverb: *If you want to go fast, go alone. If you want to go far, go together.*

Rarely in our human history have we heard of a tribe of people surviving a migration because only one person took the journey. It's been the journey together that has ensured that generations of people have survived. We don't have to simply survive this life. We can thrive in an abundance of care when we consistently operate in community—a reciprocal circle of help and support.

There are many reasons we find it difficult to ask for help. We're scared to experience the disappointment we felt in the past—unsure if we can, again, pick ourselves up after being let down. Sometimes, we're afraid of being vulnerable, and other times we might think we've not done enough to be helped. And so, we spend hours trying to find perfect solutions to our problems before seeing our therapist. We wait to get help on our draft business plan until it's "just right." And we won't hire a fitness trainer until we've lost another five pounds.

Other times, we're only so available to be helped. Too often, we don't, as my friend Luvvie says, "let our helpers find us." We hide. We can be afraid to acknowledge our full needs—even with those we trust. We're afraid to be a burden to them, but real community is built through the shared burden. It's formed in the struggle and remembered on the mountaintops. It's not that we can't do hard things alone, but what if we were never meant to?

I was so proud when I finally made enough money to hire someone to help us clean our house. However, hours before the person arrived, I instinctively started to clean my house! I was doing what my mama had trained us to do: clean it before they come. Her logic? If your house is too disorganized, people won't be able to clean it very well. Some of y'all are laughing, but this still makes sense to me. But I also know this reasoning doesn't translate to every circumstance.

In some areas of our lives, a bit of preparation may be helpful, like agendas we create before meetings. But then there are times when all we can do is show up raw, untidy, and unprepared, like when grief kicks us out of the driver's seat and simple decisions become too much for us to make. No matter the circumstance, when we need help, we can't let our fear of being seen as less capable or less worthy prevent us from asking for the support we know we need.

Receiving help can be hard, especially when we've been conditioned to believe an ugly lie: *We* are the help, so we can't receive any help. We're mothers, so it's "our job" to cook every night, even if work has us depleted. We're the oldest, so it's "up to us" to attend all of dad's doctor's appointments. But right now, I want us to confront that ugly lie with a beautiful truth: *We are worthy to be helped*. Embracing help doesn't mean we are worthless or incapable of doing hard things. It means that we recognize that we are precious.

To embrace help, we first have to believe a few things.

1) We deserve help
2) We don't have to be perfect to receive help
3) We don't have to figure it all out before we ask for help
4) We don't have to relive our trauma to be worthy of help

For some of us, our "ask muscle" is atrophied, so we need to get into the proverbial gym and lift small weights. In practice, this could be asking for help on a low-stakes task or accepting an offer of help. The next time a coworker wants to buy you coffee? Say yes! Does a friend want to babysit your kids? Let 'em! It's time for you to remember what support feels like. And just like we hire trainers or get gym buddies, we can ask a friend to hold us accountable in this area. I know some of us might have to attend to our ask trauma through therapy or coaching, and we should. We don't want our past pain to stop our future healing. Our commitment to healing will build our confidence in ourselves and others.

Embrace Your Limits

To honor our precious humanity, I want to share one more mindset that can help us practice how we meet our needs and treat ourselves with gentle hands: Know your limits.

I love sports—especially the behind the scenes that goes into an athlete's performance. In their pregame or post-event interviews, athletes will often describe how well they understood what was happening in their bodies. "I knew I had a lot left in the tank." Or "I told coach I needed a breather before the fourth quarter."

Now, I'm not here to debate your basketball GOAT, but it's no surprise why LeBron James is reported to have spent a million dollars a year on his health and conditioning. This investment has helped him understand his body and what he can demand of it. Whether it's the athletes we love, the warriors we revere, or, yes, even Jesus (it's your friendly PK tapping in again), people who perform at the highest levels *know* their bodies. We need this same kind of knowing.

We embrace our limits in reverence to our humanity. Simone Biles knows how to stretch herself when the moment calls for it. She doesn't deliver Olympic-level performances at every practice because it would harm her body. It's the same for us. We have to respect our mental, physical, emotional, and physiological capacity, knowing when we've had enough and when we can stand to go a little longer. Our self-awareness helps us to embrace our limits.

It seems counterintuitive, but there is freedom in limitations. Respecting our limits means we're not stretched thin, and only then do we have more freedom and capacity to go deeper in the areas where we are meant to invest. This is when we can begin to see a "No" as a very powerful "Yes!"

Even further, our limits can serve as protection. The truth is, we aren't meant to be everything to everyone, and we aren't meant to be everywhere, doing everything. We have limits on what we can consume and when we can consume it. We have limits on where we can go and who we can be with. This understanding is how we begin to see the soft landing in our limits.

Limitations inherently feel negative, as they often describe what's not possible, or what we can't accomplish. But what if we thought about our limits as a gate? One we could see through and open and close. With discernment, over time we need to tend to our gate, updating the hinges or changing the paint. In the same way, our limits, like our boundaries, need updating. The point of embracing our limits isn't to put a lifetime mandate on what we can or can't do. Rather, this practice is about confidently respecting our sacred capacity. The capacity that stops us from taking in, or pouring out, too much. On our hard days, and when we have very little to give, we will land softly when we remember to protect what's sacred and to embrace our limits without guilt.

We Can Do This

In a world that wants us to forget that we are sacred, the invitation to be gentle with ourselves might be the most important RSVP of our lives. When we say yes to being gentle, we're telling ourselves that we're worthy of so much. Worthy of rest, worthy of love, worthy of care, worthy of second chances . . . simply worthy. And I know that we are.

Every time we choose to be softer on ourselves, we are signaling to the Universe that we appreciate the chance to just be alive. And I know we may feel far away from the little person we once were, the little person that was so precious. But they're still in us, asking for our protection and guiding us back to our gentle hands.

An Invitation to Reflect and Act

It might be tempting to try and apply everything you just read at once, but that may not be the gentle transition you need. Here's my invitation to you: Set a timer for three minutes. During this time, I will sit with you as you think of two ways to be more gentle with yourself this week. Think of small but mighty acts. *Don't judge it before you write it. Just let it flow out of you.* Tip: Don't erase anything, just add to it.

Whatever you write down, try it with consistent effort for the next week. (You might skip a day, and that's okay! Just return to the practice.) In a journal, note any changes you see in yourself.

What are you learning?

What are you noticing?

What felt good?

What got easier with practice?

CHAPTER 2

Feel Your Feelings

Man was a feeling creature long before he was a thinking creature.

HOWARD THURMAN

Making friends as an adult is . . . interesting. Most of us, no longer in school, find ourselves questioning if that work friend can officially become a "real friend" or if the mom we met at the park is cool enough to exchange real numbers with. We've all been there. And then there are times when, in a larger friend group, you become friends with another person just because you share other friends. In most adopt-a-friend scenarios, you might not do the normal friend vetting you'd typically do. You don't think you need to because people have already vouched for them. "They're cool!" you think. So-and-so said, "She's good people!"

You know the vibes.

I've had this happen a lot, though there's a particular person that sticks out. I'll call her Megan.

In hindsight, Megan was more of a "cool work associate" than a true friend. But because of our shared background and friend circle, I assumed we were meant to be closer. Well, one day she gave me a backhanded compliment and attempted to, as the kids say, "son me" in front of other people. Some might have taken her behavior as a joke, but my intuition told me it was much more.

I brought this experience to therapy. I explained that I had clocked my so-called friend's actions. I told my therapist how I wanted to manage our relationship moving forward, how I needed to protect myself and that I would start treating this friend as an acquaintance. As expected, Dr. A held space for me as I got it all out. And then, like clockwork, she asked me to do the thing I had been avoiding:

"I hear how you want to manage this relationship, but first, let's get clear on your feelings. I know what happened. Now tell me how it made you *feel*."

I wasn't sure how to answer that.

"I really *feel* like our situation is dissolving because of her underlying insecurities and how my presence triggers them. I *feel* like we might have run our course as friends. I have seen her do this to other people, but I didn't think that it would happen to me. We've even prayed together!"

"Okay. And how did her actions make you *feel*?" my therapist asked.

I fumbled with my fingers and my eyes darted around my office for answers. When I looked back at the screen, I caught Dr. A's reassuring eye. I looked away and took a breath. *Sigh. I'm paying for her help, so I might as well tell her the truth.* After a few more steadying breaths, I began to let myself feel what was bubbling underneath the surface.

Through trembling lips, I finally said, "I am feeling disappointed, embarrassed, ashamed, and angry."

"I'm glad you shared, Jovian. Now we can get to a place of exploring what you want to do with these feelings."

I'd been doing what so many of us do: intellectualizing how we feel versus letting ourselves *feel* how we feel. We often conflate what we think with how we feel. It's more comfortable (and easier) for us to intellectualize our emotions than to actually *feel* them. Through early socialization and societal conditioning, many of us have been trained to suppress or deny our feelings—especially the "bad" ones, like anger (if you're a woman) and sadness (if you're a man). However, this is a denial of our humanity and a way to distance ourselves from who we really are.

We are not robots who build; we are humans who feel. When we deny how we feel, we are unable to advocate, protect, or attend to our human needs. This can make a hard day even harder as we lose the chance for connection and provision. When we pretend to be okay when we're not, we deny ourselves the chance to be helped, to be witnessed, to be held.

With this grounding invitation, I invite us into a soft landing where we give ourselves permission to feel, where we see our feelings as both information and a conduit for empathy and connection—not something to be repressed or ignored.

Our Feelings Are Data

All of us have feelings and emotions—some we call good, bad, or even ugly—but it's worth knowing that although most of us see them as interchangeable, they are not quite the same.

Emotions are our body's automatic response to internal and external stimuli. They are quick, instinctive physiological responses that happen without our control or conscious awareness, such as a surprised facial expression. As with many things in our body, they were designed to protect us from threats and help us survive. In a sense, our emotions send us a text like, "Hey, your chest is tight. You are afraid. Something important is happening and you need to pay attention to it." For example, sweaty palms can signal discomfort, or rapid breathing can signal surprise.

Feelings are closely related but not the same. Our feelings use our past experiences, memories, and beliefs to make a story about our emotions. When a feeling arises, it texts us like, "Hey, your palms are sweaty. We are feeling insecure and nervous because we are about to give a speech in front of five thousand people. You feel this way because someone might make fun of you, just like they did your freshman year." Some other examples are feeling awkward as a plus-one to a party or feeling confident when your teammates pick you to be their captain.

The interaction between emotions and feelings has been described as a feedback loop, where our emotions trigger an involuntary physical response that our feelings then use to create an intentional story. While we can't help our emotions, which happen to us, or always regulate our feelings, which are constructed by us, they are both crucial pieces of data that can help us identify what we truly need and want in any given moment. Of course, this requires us to first be honest with ourselves about what it is we feel.

On any given night, you could walk into my house and hear me say, "Octopus!" and have no clue what's going on. But you know who does? My daughter, Jorgie. It all started after what was a particularly long day of work. Jorgie, home from school with boundless energy, and George, done with an exciting day on set, were both eager to give me a full download. It was my night to cook, and while I seasoned the broccoli, George began telling me all about his day. Meanwhile, Jorgie begged me to watch her encore dance performance.

Before I could say anything, Jorgie started twirling and singing a song from *The Princess and the Frog*. After a minute or two, George saw what was happening and paused his download, but it was too late. My body got hot and my mind started to swirl. Right then, it was all just too much for me to focus on. Everything was loud, and it seemed like everyone was pulling on me. I suddenly felt overwhelmed. I put the seasoning back on the counter and told them I was going to the bathroom. I didn't care if the broccoli burned. I sat on the edge of the tub and took some deep breaths. What everyone needed from me in that moment was more than I had to give.

After a few minutes, I went back into the living room and told Jorgie we needed to talk. I told her, "From now on, when Mommy feels like she's getting pulled in lots of directions, like she has eight legs, she's going to say 'Octopus!' That means Mommy needs silence and time to reset."

"Okay, Mommy!" said Jorgie. She thought for a second and

replied, "And when I *really* need your attention, I'm going to say 'Jellyfish!'"

And so now, my house is an aquarium.

Before I found my way to *octopus*, there were many days when I ignored how I felt and pushed through my emotions to get the job done. I wanted to be a "good" mom, leader, or teammate. Turns out, I should have have called "Octopus!" years ago.

When we ignore our feelings, we can't respond to our real needs. We can't ask for comfort when we feel insecure, or safety when we feel afraid. In all of this, we miss the chance to treat ourselves well. This matters, because over time, we end up losing self-confidence that we can *trust and protect who we are*. How do we find a soft landing if we stop protecting ourselves? How do we honor our humanity if we can't trust ourselves to see it? Feeling our feelings helps us to do both.

As we remember our humanity and accept the invitation to honor what we feel, we see our feelings and emotions are natural parts of the human experience. To deny them is to deny our humanity. Our feelings aren't meant to be fixed. Rather, they're meant to be felt, acknowledged, and processed.

As Dr. Anita Phillips says in her *New York Times* bestselling book, *The Garden Within*, "Disconnecting from your feelings is not an act of faith; it is an act of avoidance. The unsolved pain is still there, beneath the surface, eroding your well-being." Research shows that it's the feelings we leave unattended—the shame, confusion, and even joy—that can have a negative effect on our hearts and overall well-being, manifesting in somatic symptom disorders (headaches, gastrointestinal issues, etc.) and physiological strain (prolonged states of fight or flight). We can't heal what we won't acknowledge is hurt. Our feelings need our attention.

How We Learned Not to Feel

Now, I can't speak for all of us, but a lot of Black millennials grew up hearing this phrase: "Stop crying before I give you something to cry about." If we heard this, we knew whatever was invoking our tears—our embarrassment, fear, confusion, annoyance—needed to stop. It was an inconvenience, and it needed to end immediately unless we wanted to get spanked. Sorry, parents, but I'm sure we can all agree that even though it was acceptable to say at the time, and we still laugh about it, it's cringeworthy to write about now. The sentiment of that infamous phrase? *Your feelings are a problem.*

This idea echoed throughout society when I was growing up, and it still does today. Football players get fined for celebrating in the end zone, and we've never forgotten that line from *A League of Their Own*, "There's no crying in baseball!" From the shows we watched on TGIF to the adults we saw trying to control their praise at church, we noticed how expressing our emotions could be to our detriment. We saw some mock President Barack Obama for crying during a press conference held for a heinous school shooting, while other leaders who remained blank-faced were said to exhibit poise. Time and again a message was reinforced: *Your feelings are inconvenient. Your feelings should be tamed.*

For many of us, we've grown up professionally fearing retribution for acknowledging our feelings at work. We're worried we'll be seen as too sensitive, too angry, hyperemotional, or not a credible leader. In our careers, roles associated with the emotional and psychological well-being of a team, like "being the culture setter" or "moral leader," are deemed soft skills and often underappreciated. Those of us who thrive in these spaces are often relegated to departments with leaner budgets, less resources, and lower exposure. But here's a thought: *If our skills are so soft, why does everyone bring us their hardest problems to fix?*

Then there's the role of gender. Gender rules confine all of us in inhumane prisons, and the ripple effects are cataclysmic. So many cishet men in positions of influence and power grow up emotionally stunted, unable and unwilling to identify their feelings, specifically sadness, disappointment, or embarrassment. And expressing vulnerability? Out of the question. This, of course, impacts how these men move through the world, the people they lead, the cultural norms they enforce, and the people who would choose to partner with them, whether platonic or romantically.

Though we're often lauded for being caregivers of culture and the emotional centers of our communities, as women we're told we shouldn't feel *too* much. This is especially true for Black Women. Our decorum matters more than our comfort. We can only feel once everyone and everything has been attended to. When our likability has been tied to our output, the "shoulds" dominate our decision-making. We don't want to inconvenience others, so we should stay quiet. We don't want to "make a fuss," so we should internalize our annoyance and resentment. The cycle continues, and our bodies and mental health pay the price.

Unfortunately, when we believe our feelings are a problem, we often end up falling into a feeling that disconnects us from ourselves and others: shame.

The Shadow of Shame

Have you ever felt ashamed for feeling what you feel? Yep, me too. It's like the day you feel ignored by your friends. You drop big news in the group chat and no one replies. Four minutes later, in the same chat, someone sends a viral video and another person a link for Girl Scout cookies. Before you know it, your big news is buried and people have moved on to weekend plans or Thin Mints. The experience itself stings, but you deny it. *It's silly*, you think, *I should be more mature than to feel hurt by this.* It's hard to admit that you feel upset about something "so small." But now you don't just feel hurt. You feel ashamed for feeling hurt. This is what happens when we've been shamed into thinking that we have to be stronger than our feelings.

I want us to give ourselves permission to feel, without judgment, what's inconvenient, small, or not ideal. So many of us are covered in blankets of shame, hiding from what we feel. We ask ourselves:

Am I still a good mom if I have days when I hate all the tasks that come along with motherhood?

Being a caretaker wasn't a part of my plan. Am I allowed to grieve the life I thought I would have? Is there space for me to feel lonely and not just "grateful" when I'm in a relationship where my partner travels 50 percent of the time?

Should I just ignore the grief and anger I have over friends who left me once my career took off? Should I just be happy that I made it?

It's been nine years since my mom died but the grief still feels fresh. Is it okay that I'm not over it?

We wonder these things in desperation, wanting to not be shamed for these feelings or convinced they don't matter, but we too often still carry the shame. Our soft landing comes when we remember that our emotions and feelings keep us human. They are not an afterthought or a mistake—they are our actual human design! And yes, we can work to strengthen our emotional regulation while we still remember that our bodies will have automatic responses to stimuli we can't control. Shaming ourselves for the human experience of "emoting" is not just counterintuitive, but it's also damaging and dehumanizing to our very way of being.

For years, with limited help, my friend Josh cared for his mother. As she aged, she at times became mean and difficult to care for. When I would ask how he was doing, he would tell me he was sorry for her. And even though she could be mean and unforgiving, he knew he shouldn't let a seventy-eight-year-old woman get on his nerves. What Josh didn't realize was that there's no age limit to causing harm. I can hear my therapist now: "Old people can still hurt your feelings."

Things continued until, one day, Josh snapped and yelled at his mom. Ashamed, he then locked himself in the bathroom, desperately trying to compose himself. The feelings he'd ignored finally bubbled to the surface. Before then, he never let himself acknowledge what he really felt: angry, disrespected, lonely, and powerless.

Suppression stops healing. Safe expression invites it. Our feelings, whatever they are, matter.

Our Feelings Are a Bridge

Acknowledging our true feelings is the vulnerable practice of allowing ourselves to become undone. In the undone, we care less about performing the right thing and more about witnessing our truth. We don't worry about what they say we should feel. We just let ourselves feel what's true, even if it's inconvenient. We say, "*Yes, I'm disgusted,*" "*Yes, I feel betrayed,*" or "*Yes, I feel proud.*" When we acknowledge our feelings, whether it's grief or sheer joy, we clear a path to genuine empathy and human connection. Our feelings can be a bridge—connecting us to the world around us and the people in it.

Lily (aka Lils) has been one of my best friends since we were in college. Pretty inseparable since the day we met, Lily and I took the University of North Carolina by storm. But for me, it wasn't our late nights partying or even our campaign strategy sessions that cemented our bond. That would happen one year post-graduation when I called Lily with some news that would change my life.

When I called, Lily was on set, working as a coveted NBC page.

"What's up, Jo?" she whispered hurriedly. "We're live so I can't talk long."

"Okay, okay. I gotta tell you some good news! I got a promotion and I'm moving to New York."

Now, I don't know what Lily's coworkers *saw,* but what I *heard* was the kind of screaming and foot thumping that would typically happen at a party, not when you're standing thirty feet from a live show.

She burst into tears. "Joooooooo!!!! Oh my gosh, oh my gosh!!! I am so happy!!!"

"Thank you Lils!!! Wait, where are you again?!"

"I don't even know! I'm crying under a random desk! I'm just so happy for you!!!"

Her environment may not have been the ideal space for her to feel her true feelings, but she felt them anyway. As we hung up, I burst into tears, too, so touched that she was so happy. After that moment, I knew, come hell or high water, I'd never let our friendship go. And how could I? Lily came undone for me. Our deeper connection, just like our first one, was forged through vulnerability.

The process of acknowledging and then sharing our feelings is how we've always built meaningful relationships. It's like when we used to stay up late talking to our friends at sleepover camp. As we hung over our bunks, we told one another how we really felt about school, our parents, or the people we liked. We immediately felt closer to one another. We knew we would sit together at breakfast and the conversations would continue from the canteen to the campfire. Our choice to feel, and to feel honestly and openly, was what brought us closer as friends.

As we have aged, our ability to feel our feelings has continued to open the door to connection. This matters because we need people to know us so we can better know ourselves. This takes a reciprocal unveiling and unmasking. The relationships that we treasure most are the ones where we've agreed to bear witness to our shared humanity. In these precious unions, we've agreed to imperfectly hold each other's messy, complicated, "all over the feelings wheel" type of stuff that makes us authentically *us*. These become the sacred relationships that create a gorgeous tapestry to backdrop our lives. These relationships comfort us when we're in sorrow, and they match our joy when we're on the mountaintop. Connected by our feelings, these relationships breed empathy and help us become more fully alive, more fully human. They give us a soft landing.

Grace to Feel Again: Ways We Can Feel Our Feelings

We may not have heard our grandmothers say they felt disillusioned or our fathers admit that they felt afraid. And for some of us, this caused real harm, harm we're now tending to as adults. To help us land softly as we continue to heal, let's view their experience with grace. Because of grace, we can imagine that they were doing the best they could with what they had at the time. But we won't stay there. With grace, now we can build from their imperfect efforts, knowing there's a better way forward. As we raise the next generation, we can show them how to boldly accept the soft landing of feeling our feelings as a way of honoring our humanity. Here are some ways to start.

Start with Grace and Support

Grace is the gift that keeps giving. With grace, we can find forgiveness for what we were unable to feel earlier. And with grace, we can find the resilience to trust ourselves again. Remembering grace will help us release judgment and find new truths.

And of course, because we don't have to do this alone, we can engage in tactical practices like therapy, somatic healing, and coaching to help us better feel our feelings along the way. In these confidential and safe spaces, we can address the big *T* and little *t* trauma that impacts our overall emotional well-being.

Practice Positive Curiosity

Positive curiosity, an aspect of emotional intelligence, helps us discover our truths without judgment. Dr. Summer Allen, an emotional intelligence expert and researcher says positive curiosity is a mindset that involves a sequence of reflective questions to enhance self-awareness, social awareness, and emotional intelligence.

When you find yourself overcome with an emotion, here are some reflection questions that prompt positive curiosity:

- What thoughts are bubbling to the surface?
- When, if ever, have I experienced something like this before? Felt this before? What is similar or different?

- How is my body impacting how I feel? How have I been sleeping? What meals have I eaten today?
- What specific event or interaction triggered this emotion?

Space for discovery interrupts impulsive judgment. When we get to know ourselves without judgment, we become more fully honest with who we are. Over time, we begin to better process and respond to our feelings while developing strong self-trust. Positive curiosity is a powerful tool to support self-awareness and regulation, not emotional suppression.

Use an Emotions Wheel

An Emotions Wheel, also commonly referred to as a Feelings Wheel, is an accessible tool that helps us locate how we might feel in any given moment. There are so many ways to describe how we really feel. Instead of the standard emotional designation of angry, happy, or sad, an emotions wheel helps us to deepen our self-awareness by expanding our emotional vocabulary. Imagine a friend asks, "How are you?" and instead of replying, "I'm good," you say, "I'm feeling content and valued." Now which reply do you think sparks more conversation? Freely available online, this is a great tool to print off and use with your family or close friends. For example, keep the wheel in the middle of the dinner table. As you all discuss the day, the wheel is passed around as everyone answers the question, "Name one memorable thing from today. How did it make you feel and why?"

Here are some words you can use to expand your emotional vocabulary:

Content
Discontent
Betrayed
Playful
Valued
Numb

Journal Your Feelings

There's one line in Mark Batterson's book, *Draw the Circle*, that I'll never forget. "The shortest pencil is longer than the longest memory." Honest journaling preserves your history. This matters as our feelings are important but fleeting. By capturing our stories, one-line entries, or doodles, we give the gift of memory to our future selves. Journaling gives us powerful insight into who we are and who we are becoming. Our journals can be our private canvases where we make sense of what we're experiencing. They are our place to discover what's going on in our mind, body, and spirit. Journaling as an intentional practice helps us not only to feel our feelings, but to expand our self-awareness. Sometimes, our journals are the safest place for us to process our emotions. And unlike social media, they are where we can see the truth of how we feel without the weight of another person's judgment.

There are no rules for your journal. It's where you can pick apart ideas, test theories, and rationalize your desires. It's your private escape. You can call it whatever you want: diary, messy place . . . whatever you name it, just make it yours!

Feel with People You Trust

Every Wednesday I gather on FaceTime with three of my oldest college friends. For an hour, we talk about everything from family and health to new hobbies and college memories. We make space for the serious and the silly. We embody what it means to hold each other in gracious accountability and loving support. With every tear we shed and honest emotion we express, our bond is further cemented. Even better for us, we do this call on the move—each agreeing to walk while we talk. This helps us unlock even more vulnerability because we're lowering our cortisol (the body's stress hormone) with our movement. Being less stressed helps us to be more honest and open.

Who do you feel safe with? It doesn't have to be a long list. Identify those people and practice emotional vulnerability with them. Start small. For instance, if your partner cancels plans you were looking forward to, text your friend to say how disappointed you are. The next time you're in a movie theater, don't stifle your laugh. Instead, let yourself come alive and *feel* the funny. This might seem small and intuitive, and even a little like, "Duh, Jovian." But I bet you're living far more constrained than you even realize. As you build your feelings muscle, raise the stakes. When a new friend asks how you're doing, give them the honest answer versus the reflexive, "I'm good." Lead with the vulnerability you want to experience with other people.

Do you have relationships that need to develop more emotional safety? Start by practicing more active listening, reflection, and consistency in conversations and experiences. While in conversation, maintain eye contact, use engaging body language, reflect what you hear, and confirm that you understand (if you do). If you don't understand, ask questions with positive curiosity, not judgment. Show your consistency by following through on your word, and if things change, let people know early—not after you've missed a deadline or commitment.

We Can Do This

Our world's ever-increasing pace has conditioned us to outrun, suppress, or avoid our humanity. But our emotions and feelings keep us human. When we're attuned to them, we can better understand what we need to get through some of life's hardest days—the days we need space to grieve, and the days we need a hand to hold because someone took their heart away from ours. When we're aware of how we feel, we can help ourselves find the soft landing that will bring us back home.

An Invitation to Reflect and Act

We're so used to denying or pushing through our feelings that we may have to build new comfort and safety with knowing how we feel. Comfort comes from familiarity, and that familiarity comes with practice. We're invited to start reflecting and feeling our feelings right now. As you're ready, spend time answering these two questions.

At this moment I am feeling ________________________.

I am feeling this way because ________________________.

CHAPTER 3

Believe You Are Worthy

Deal with yourself as an individual worthy of respect and make everyone else deal with you the same way.

NIKKI GIOVANNI

My college friend Meena is like so many of us. Ambitious, intentional, and after years of hard work, now a trusted voice in her field. Our group text buzzed with hearts and clapping memes when she sent us this message:

"I did it y'all. I'm officially the new senior vice president!"

This promotion made Meena the youngest woman at her company to ever have the role, and it came with high stakes. Her company was on the other side of a recent merger, and her team had a limited runway to hit new goals. Thankfully, her boss loved her, and her direct reports were a mix of people she'd recruited or mentored over time. She felt confident and set up for success. But as it is with all of us, she'd have days when her confidence would dip and she'd question her value.

Now a senior leader, Meena was a member of the executive leadership team (ELT) and expected to attend new meetings. Before her first ELT meeting, she changed into her favorite shirt and hyped herself up in the bathroom. As she settled into her seat, she looked around the table, noting many of the leaders she'd admired over the years. But she also noticed that there was no one else like her in the room. This wasn't new for her, and typically, she could manage it, but today felt different. As her eyes darted around the room, she subconsciously began to size up her peers. Soon, she was doing internal math; compared to everyone else, her years of experience didn't feel like enough. She started to get antsy, feeling new pressure. She had to deliver, and she had to do it now. People were counting on her. In the span of five minutes, her excitement gave way to a flood of doubts. *Do I even belong here? I knew I needed one more year to prepare. What if they don't respect my strategy? What if I can't handle this?*

To hear Meena tell it, it was only by grace that she was able to reel herself in from the deep end of self-doubt. She told us, "If it had been three years earlier, I probably wouldn't have said much in the meeting, thinking I didn't belong there. But somehow, I kept whispering to myself, *This is my space now. I'm where I'm meant to be.*"

Meena's whispers are a reminder: *Our self-talk matters.* Our positive beliefs and powerful inner dialogue can help us find grace and confidence on the days we question our value—or let our doubts demand that we stop showing up. Those hard days will come, and when they do, we are invited to land softly by believing we are worthy.

We've all experienced self-doubt, whether in a new career, relationship, or even when it's been our turn to host Christmas dinner. The doubts themselves aren't the problem—it's when these doubts become fully formed beliefs that dehumanize us, making us believe we can never rest, make mistakes, or deserve life's goodness. These limiting beliefs can make us work ourselves into oblivion or stop us from taking up space that's rightfully ours. They can interfere with our imaginations and harass our dreams. But today, our soft landing is inviting us to believe that we are good, capable, and *worthy* of infinite possibilities.

What Do You Believe?

We all carry beliefs. It's a function of how our brains operate. Some of our beliefs are good, stretching us toward what seems impossible. Others are negative and constricting—relegating us to small lives and limited exposure. Our beliefs impact our personal and professional growth. They can be the reason why we don't advocate for ourselves, or why we settle in relationships. If we carry the belief, "I am a burden," we might not even tell a waiter that they gave us the wrong meal. Or, if we believe that parenthood is a form of martyrdom, we might feel overwhelming guilt when we want to take a trip without our children. Our limiting beliefs can prevent us from self-advocating, meeting new people, and creating healthy boundaries.

In the same way that we carry beliefs that limit our possibilities, we also carry beliefs that expand them. Beliefs like, "I can make mistakes and learn from them," are why some of us find it easy to try new things. And beliefs like, "I'm a good friend," are why we won't let ourselves stay in friendships that have become unhealthy. Our beliefs inform our care.

It's hard to experience a soft landing when we are consistently hard on ourselves, shortchanging our dreams, or diminishing our worth because we don't believe we're deserving. And all of us, often unknowingly, can operate out of limiting beliefs.

How many times have we stopped ourselves from applying to a job because we undervalued our experience? Limiting belief. Spun ourselves into a web of paralysis overthinking an idea because it's not "perfect?" Limiting belief. These constricting beliefs discourage us from asking for what we deserve and convince us to settle for a beginner's salary when we should be demanding the expert's. Limiting beliefs block our progress and blindfold us to our greatness. They question our inherent worthiness.

Some of us are so conditioned to question our worthiness that we've stopped believing in our own capacity for goodness. Before we know it, we've stopped giving ourselves permission to rest, time to heal, and optionality to fail. We've at times allowed others to treat us similarly, tolerating the bare minimum, removing our boundaries, and sticking around for disrespect, even abuse.

When we find ourselves questioning our inherent value and second-guessing our goodness, our work is adopting new mindsets that say: *I am worthy and I embody goodness.* This may require re-narrating our lives, or unpacking our internal scripts in the safety of a clinical relationship. When we reconstitute our worthiness, we remind ourselves that we can believe in ourselves. As we challenge limiting beliefs, we reassert that we deserve the good in this life. It's how we adopt a new internal script: *I reject the limits they put on my greatness.*

Saying yes to our worthiness is how we live into the fullness of our purpose, honor the truth of our identity, and give ourselves the space to fail, learn, and grow. It's how we grant ourselves the comfort of a soft landing in hard times. It looks like finding resolve when we question if we belong in the room and self-esteem on the days we're tempted to turn down love. It's how we destroy limiting beliefs one by one.

This is shape-shifting work, and it begins by identifying the origin of our limiting beliefs.

Where Do Our Beliefs Come From?

Our beliefs come from many places. Some were born at home with our primary caregivers, while others matured as we consumed mass media and navigated teachers' opinions and dysfunctional work environments. From popular culture to unspoken family expectations, how we internalize our value is often distorted through the eyes of others. We've had family members who, even in their good intentions to protect us, passed down limiting beliefs through respectability politics.

"We don't do things like . . ."

"Don't draw attention to yourself."

"You need to work twice as hard to get half as far."

"Don't let them see you sweat."

"You're the _____ one; you can't act like that."

"Good girls/boys don't do stuff like that."

If like me you've started to unpack these as an adult, it's fair to say we've kept our therapists busy, right?

Along with family, many of our limiting beliefs have come from the injurious structural and institutional policies that have put our identities on the margins and subjugated our worth to public discussion. Every "-ism," from racism and ableism to sexism, heterosexism, and classism, has systematically dehumanized us—underscoring that we can't believe in the fullness of our humanity without challenging these systems. After all, these ideologies have birthed, swaddled, and raised many of our generational beliefs.

Early in my career, I worked as a fundraiser for a national nonprofit. This often required talking to high-net-worth individuals. During a conversation at one of our events, a donor questioned my education and professional experiences. In the moment, I stood my ground, challenged the microaggression, and de-escalated the interaction with textbook precision. I'd been trained to anticipate this pain—but it didn't mean it didn't hurt like hell. I excused myself from the conversation and I escaped to the bathroom on the brink of tears. I stared in the mirror through tear-filled eyes as thoughts battled in my head: *He's telling me I don't deserve to be here. . . . He thinks I'm not enough. . . . But of course I belong here! . . . I'm fearfully and wonderfully made. . . . I'm Nat and Chandra's daughter. . . . I'm God's beloved child.*

I bet you've had this type of inner dialogue, too. Many of us who are deemed unworthy by society are constantly warding off dehumanizing thoughts. The connection between our beliefs and society's oppressive systems matters. It highlights who can more easily accept the invitation to believe they're worthy. *While others may accept this invitation as a method of thriving, some of us have to accept it just to survive.* When we live with systemically oppressed identities we need this soft landing more than ever.

Some limiting beliefs come from past trauma and form as adaptive survival learning. It's why a child who dealt with abandonment might carry thoughts like, *I must be perfect or else they'll leave.* Or *They'll disappear again if I ask for something.* These childhood experiences form beliefs that can produce hyper-independence, hypervigilance, and limiting beliefs.

Some of our limiting beliefs are reinforced by the injustice we've witnessed or experienced firsthand at work. For instance, you were overqualified for a job but still passed over for Scott, who has less experience and a record of creating psychologically unsafe environments. Over time, experiences like these can chip away at our confidence and make us question our voice, expertise, and right to vulnerability.

Culture shapes our limiting beliefs and how we understand the world around us. As the internet continues to be the main conduit for how we share news, culture, and information, how we see ourselves will be shaped by filtered realities. This impacts our beliefs, as more and more we perceive life's complicated truths as simplistic stories, and we become unnecessarily anxious about our paths to success, and what people "like us" can do.

Why Do We Hold On to Some of Our Limiting Beliefs?

It's annual review time, and Jordan sits down with their manager ready to go over their goals and results. Jordan's manager gives them the highest rating possible, with 95 percent of the review being overwhelmingly positive. The manager gave Jordan one piece of constructive feedback, but all the way home, it was the only thing Jordan could think about.

Raise your hand if you've been Jordan. (I just raised both of mine.) We tend to remember the negative. The dinner party was a smashing success, but you're still thinking about the spring rolls you forgot to serve. In moments like these, why do you hold on to the negative?

It's not just you; it's all of us. As an evolutionary survival measure, our brains are predisposed to focus on the negative, or what is called a negativity bias. Our distant ancestors were once challenged by environmental threats—i.e., predators—so attention to negative stimuli was imperative for survival. This inclined response to negativity has stayed with us, and it means we're more likely to remember how to avoid getting hurt than we are to remember how to spot the good. This translates to our beliefs, as we are neurologically hardwired to lean into conversations with our internal critics and volley negative, hypercritical self-talk before engaging in positive self-talk.

Humans, we are so complicated.

At times we hold on to some old beliefs because we want to avoid uncertainty and a lack of control. Our preference is to remain close to what is familiar, even if the familiar is harmful. Our brains love comfort, and so it is, in effect, scary to our brains to challenge old beliefs, even if those old beliefs say limiting things like, *I have to earn love*, or *I don't deserve rest*. These beliefs then become stories we tell ourselves, and as a way of avoiding the unknown and seemingly predicting the future, we act into these beliefs and confirm what we believed to be true. This is how confirmation bias—the tendency to search for and interpret information that confirms previous beliefs—shows up.

Our awareness of why our brains have and hold on to our beliefs is an important step to finding paths of disruption and meaningful self-regulation. But it's not just what we believe on an individual level. When we zoom out, we can see what beliefs have been passed down at scale.

Society Designed Our Doubts

Those of us with historically or legally marginalized identities know what it's like to be forced into the small corners of society. Oppressive ideologies weave through the fabric of our culture and legal system, and through the messages we receive from teachers, the media, and even at home. Whether through identity politics or unjust structural norms, we've experienced relentless attacks on our self-esteem. As a result, we've too often adopted mindsets that shrink our humanity and constrict our capacity for goodness. And when we do carry a sense of divine confidence, we're often met with skepticism—and as a way of taming us, pushed toward false humility. With all of this, it's no surprise why we often think things like: *I don't have time to fail. I'll lose my value if I don't work. It's selfish for me to say no. Am I too old to begin again? What if someone's done it better? Do I really deserve my success?*

Did that sound familiar? Feel familiar?

How often do we let our fears make our decisions? Not just our fear of failure or our fear of rejection, but the fear that whispers,

What if I deserve more? What if we believed that we are *that* powerful, *that* kind, *that* resourceful, *that* creative? What would we be then?

What's possible if we believe that we're truly worthy of it all?

Sometimes we hold on to our limiting beliefs because we know that a full belief in our worthiness means that we'll have to stop playing small. We'll let go of destructive habits that keep us comfortable, and we'll challenge ideas that keep us restricted. What if we imagined a world where our worthiness was our launchpad to a new form of liberation and freedom? The possibilities of our greatness can feel overwhelming. But this is when we must say to ourselves, *I was made for my big life. I was made worthy.*

What if our most inspiring figures never believed in their worthiness? What's a world where Toni Morrison didn't believe she could write *The Bluest Eye*? Where Stevie Wonder didn't believe enough to create *Innervisions*? Our legends weren't immune to self-doubt, but thank God they never let their doubts stop them.

What we believe informs what we do. A belief that we're worthy is how we remember to care for ourselves as we also give from ourselves. It deters us from self-harm and reminds us to lean into self-compassion and kindness. This doesn't just impact us individually; it affects everyone around us. When we believe we are worthy, we protect our light and let it shine. And along the way, we give other people permission to do the same.

Ways to Believe You Are Worthy

Of my five soft landing invitations, believing you are worthy requires a unique sense of urgency and grit. That's because it is necessarily confrontational, inspiring a confident rejection of the mindsets that dehumanize us. This is a life-preserving call to action.

Below are three ways we can accept this soft landing invitation.

Notice, Name, Be Curious, and Challenge

A few years ago, I developed a framework to help my clients expand their emotional intelligence and challenge their limiting beliefs. It's called the *Notice—Name—Be Curious—Challenge (NNCC)* framework. I'll walk you through each step using the story of my client Devin.

Devin, a fifteen-year executive in the entertainment field, was approached by a prestigious university with a job offer to be a visiting professor in their business school. Devin was shocked! While they were proud of their career, they found themselves floored by the offer to the point of disbelief, ultimately leading to feelings of unworthiness. They researched the faculty, and with every bio they read, they felt even more undeserving of the opportunity. In their mind, they weren't credentialed or degreed enough to match up to the rest of the faculty.

Here is how Devin applied the NNCC framework:

Notice: They slowed down and observed the thoughts and emotions they were having about the job. Their thoughts: *I am not as qualified as the other faculty members*. Their feelings: *insecurity and worry.*

Name: Devin named the limiting belief that was impacting their emotions and actions: *I have not done enough to deserve this opportunity.*

Be Curious: They then asked, without judgment:

- "What am I worried about?" *That I won't be good enough, and that I will fail in this new job.*
- "Why do I feel insecure?" *I don't have the same level of formal education as some of the other faculty.*
- "What story am I telling myself about myself?" *That I will always have to do more to deserve more. That I am too old to start over in a new place.*
- "How accurate are these thoughts?" *They are not the full truth.*

Challenge: Finally, Devin took time to challenge their limiting belief with the truth: *They came to me because they thought I was qualified right now. Why would they waste their time and credibility? I can address my insecurities by better understanding the job responsibilities and being mentally prepared to take* *any necessary courses or coaching to level up if needed.*

Devin made a list of evidence that was contrary to their limiting beliefs, including their accomplishments, relevant experience, values, and things they've overcome. Then, Devin synthesized it all into a powerful liberating truth: *My experience, growth mindset, and unique perspective make me a valuable asset to any team or organization.*

After working through this framework, Devin accepted the job offer with not only renewed confidence but also a plan. They reminded themself that they were a constant learner, and that anything they needed to know to do their job well, they were more than capable of learning.

We challenge our limiting beliefs with asset-based language and reframe them into our **empowering truths.** Here are two examples of common limiting beliefs and how we can challenge them.

Example 1: **Limiting Belief:** *I can't ask for help. I should know better (or this) by now.*

Notice your thoughts and emotions: *People think of me as an expert. I feel uncertain, worried, and fearful to make a mistake.*
Name the limiting belief: *Asking for help is a sign of weakness.*
Be Curious: *What's the best thing that can happen? What is within my control? What is important to me? What am I afraid of? How valid is that fear?*

Challenge: *I'm worthy of growth and learning. I don't need to have all the answers all the time.*
Empowering Truth: *I'm a lifelong learner. Asking questions signals my curiosity and commitment to growth.*

Example 2: **Limiting Belief:** *I'm not talented enough.*

Notice your thoughts and emotions: *I don't think I'm as good as everyone else. I feel nervous and inadequate.*
Name your limiting belief: *I have to be as talented as everyone else. My skill always needs to match theirs.*
Be Curious: *What story am I telling myself? That my talent isn't as good? That there's more value in what others have and who they are?*
Challenge: *My gifts and talents are unique and important. They create a positive impact.*
Empowering Truth: *I don't have to have their talent to be talented. I'll continue to expand my skills and creativity at my own pace.*

Let the People You Love Clean Your Mirror

Believing you're worthy isn't a solo venture; it's something you can, and should, do often with your trusted community. Your healing is in your sharing. By sharing your limiting beliefs, you can invite the compassion and caring accountability that will help you evolve. This looks like calling on the friend who helps us negotiate a job offer or the sister who hypes us up before a first date.

Some of us are trying to see ourselves clearly in a dirty mirror—each limiting belief adding smudges to the glass. When you can't clean the mirror yourself, I encourage you to turn to your loved ones. Ask them to clean your mirror! You might say to them, "I'm not believing in myself right now. What greatness do you see when you look at me?"

Sometimes we need other people to tell us when we're playing small or denying our possibilities. Our community can help us spot a limiting belief and, in love, help us challenge it. You know that project you've been holding on to because you're worried it's not good enough to share? I dare you to send it to your inner circle right now. I bet they'll tell you it was good enough three edits ago!

Here are some other ways you can tap into community:

- **Ask for evidence:** Ask them things like, "What are my strengths?" "Where should I give myself more credit?" "Where am I playing small?"
- **Ask for thoughtful feedback:** Ask people you trust to help you grow in a particular area: "How can I do this better next time?"
- **Borrow courage and belief:** Internalize the mindset of your biggest cheerleader and talk to yourself like they would talk to you. As my BFF IJ says, "Talk nicely to my friend!"

Protect Your Divine Inner Child

The moment we remember we are dearly beloved children is the moment we return to unconditional love. Deep inside, we all have our inner child. Psychologist Carl Jung says our inner child is a part of our subconscious mind that drives feelings and reactions stemming back from our positive or negative childhood experiences. Our inner child needs to know they're worthy. They need our love and protection, the kind that will relentlessly audit what we consume. As many of us are starting to realize, social media isn't the friend we need when we're already feeling insecure. As we love our inner child ever more, we'll turn off podcasts, delete apps, and end conversations that compel us to question our worth. Our spirit is susceptible and our inner child is too precious to be left unprotected. Our protection is in the affirmations we embody, the positive messages we consume, and the negative influences we avoid.

We Are Chosen

The invitation to believe you are worthy is your invitation to return home. It's your chance to take up space you were always designed to inhabit. It's how you embody your sense of purpose and create ripples of positive impact. As a practice, it ensures that we live into the significance of our lives, and that we give ourselves the chance to try, fail, learn, achieve, explore, rest, hurt, heal, *and* celebrate.

I know it's exhausting, navigating the insult grenades and insidious microaggressions so present in our daily experiences. It all wears on us, and sometimes we're tired of doing the work to simply believe in ourselves. But if there's anything in this life worth fighting for, it's this. We owe it to who we were, who we are now, and who we'll be. Link arms with a friend as you say to one another, "you are worthy." It may be hard to challenge the beliefs that constrict our humanity, but we know that challenge is worth our fight.

Deep in our souls, we know we've always been worthy. The Divine demanded we exist, and so now we're **here.** Who are we to argue with that? As we live each day, doing our best to understand our world and our place within it, may we always remember that we were born worthy.

An Invitation to Reflect and Act

If you had to give yourself one new, expansive truth, what would it be? *Let love guide your answer.*

Here are a few questions to support your reflection:

What do I deserve?
What have I always wanted to give myself?
What do I need?
What do I need to believe about myself to live into my purpose?
What is on the other side of my belief?

Empowering Truth: ______________________________

____

CHAPTER 4

Honor the Seasons of Your Life

Be water, my friend.

BRUCE LEE

I've always loved the telltale signs of autumn—the green leaves that turn a warm amber, and the crisp breeze that'll kiss your cheek on a morning walk. As a child, our family's commute to church along Winston-Salem's stretch of Interstate 40 was memorable. The vibrant treescape was breathtaking, even to a preoccupied teenager. Whether it's WHAM's "Last Christmas" playing in the grocery store or strawberries making their debut in spring, each new season comes with signs that it's arrived. It's the same in our lives, though at times these signs may be a bit more nuanced.

MY PHONE RANG with an incoming call from my friend Kendra.

I mused to myself, *I'm surprised she's calling. Isn't she still on her honeymoon?*

The moment I heard Kendra's voice, I knew something was wrong. She'd landed off cloud nine and real life was taking off.

"Sis, we just got home and I'm already kind of freaking out. How am I supposed to do it all?! Paul and I said we'd spend all this time together when we got back, but I gotta help my niece with her admissions stuff and we have a ton of school visits. My mom still depends on my checks every month, which means I had to commit to a bunch of work travel. I feel so stretched! I need more time to adjust."

Her voice began to crack. "To be honest, I feel like I'm failing at everything. I feel like I'm not a good wife, daughter, or aunt, and if I can't work, everything might crumble."

The floodgates opened, and she began to cry. I held her pain in our shared silence and through her occasional sniffs. After a few minutes I offered, "Ken, what if things have changed? What if you're not supposed to do it all?"

"What do you mean, Jovi?"

"Okay, let's start here. What feels most important for you to focus on right now?" I ventured.

"I'm afraid to say it," she answered hesitantly.

"No judgment, sis. I'm with you," I encouraged.

". . . Jovi, I still can't believe I'm married. I don't have a lot of examples of what a healthy marriage looks like . . . but I'm gonna get this right. I feel like, right now, I need to spend more time with Paul. But sis, if I do focus more on my marriage, I'm afraid I'll let everyone else down."

The tension in her competing commitments was becoming clear. "I feel you, sis! You just got married. Of course you wanna focus on that. Your marriage is like an infant, and it needs you. You and Paul are building your foundation, and it sounds like you're entering into a new season. And whether you anticipated it or not, you need and *want* space and time to build something special."

For weeks, the conversation with Kendra echoed in my mind. Hints of her emotional tension were suddenly mirrored in other friends and even my own life. Kendra's feelings of worry were like Morgan's feelings of resentment as a new stepmom struggling with a sudden change in morning routine. And Morgan's resentment was like my feeling of frustration as my body declined my attempts to return to long-distance running. Though rooted in different circumstances, our feelings were all sourced from the same friction that often comes with a change in season. The surprise demands of new priorities. The disappointing reality of our fragile bandwidth.

Honoring our seasons invites us to land softly by resetting our priorities and expectations to meet the moment and to remember ourselves with love in the process.

By definition we know a season to be "a time characterized by a particular circumstance or feature." With this insight we see that as the circumstances in our lives change, they also often reflect the emergence of a new season. In reverence to this, in his book, *Meditations of the Heart*, renowned mystic Howard Thurman offers us these words:

I will sing a new song. As difficult as it is, I must learn the new song that is capable of meeting the new need. I must fashion new words born of all the new growth of my life, my mind and my spirit.

It takes a lot of energy, time, and effort to transition into a new season of life, often more than we recognize. And certainly, if we're coming out of survival mode it can be even harder to get our footing—to feel stable and to make sense of what's next. The promise of our soft landing is fulfilled the more we help ourselves become aware of our changing seasons and what they mean for the intricacies of our lives. It can look like renegotiating responsibilities and demoting old desires. New seasons, no matter their size, are often marked by things like changes in a career or relationship, graduations, death, birth of an idea or child, new physical limitations, or modulations in capabilities or interests.

For Kendra, I was a voice of reason, a space to first recognize, and then later process, the realities of her new season and how she would handle her new competing commitments with the same twenty-four hours. As our lives evolve, we need trusted space, whether with our journal, friend, or coach, to attune to our feelings and needs. Without this space, it's easy to miss when a new season has arrived and to underestimate its impact. And because we're trained to keep going, to add instead of subtract, when a new season arrives, we often unmaliciously overextend ourselves, pushing past our limits and creating harm to our bodies and spirits. But I've learned we can land softly in a new season when we honor it with readjusted boundaries and priorities.

If we're lucky, we'll live such a full life that there will be many times when we're invited to rearrange our responsibilities and create space for new commitments. But there's a back room to this type of blessed life: the place where we often wrestle with our hidden guilt, resentment, or worry. At times the strain between seasons brings a swirl of questions and realizations: *I don't want the same things anymore. Why can't I keep up? What happens if I say no? Am I wrong for wanting something new? Am I less capable? Am I not grateful?* We feel the stress in all of this—the undercurrent of change pushing us to let things go, pick stuff up—evolve into something new.

Signs of Change

We've heard ourselves say it: *I just can't do it like I used to,* or *I need something more.*

We've felt our bodies tell us: *I'm too tired. I'm uninspired,* or even, *I'm finally feeling settled.*

THE MOMENT KENDRA returned from her honeymoon she felt tense, ashamed, and physically pressed on all sides. She woke every day braced to carry her load. It wasn't the way she wanted to live and it showed in her rising blood pressure, suppressed tears, and constantly clenched fists.

We usually don't have to look far beyond our bodies to know that a season has changed. It's like realizing you're suddenly lactose intolerant. (Whew, chile!) It's knowing you just can't hang like you used to, because now you need a whole weekend to recover from one night out! We get signals of a new season—the recurring headache, or newly settled nervous system, the surge of refreshed energy . . . they're lights on our bodies' dashboards, telling us to check our capacity, goals, and focus.

Maybe we've entered a season of deep contentment, appreciating how the beauty of our mundane routine settles our nervous system. Or maybe this is our time to press into an old dream, finally making time to study for the LSAT.

Life meets us where we are, always inviting us to discover who else we might become . . . now. Who will we be when we start dating again, try a new hobby, or go to bed earlier? Each season is etched with possibilities to expand our understanding of life and our role within it.

Step into Deeper Self-Awareness

Are you in a new season? Do you sense one is coming? When you're ready, use these questions to help you discover if you're in, or preparing to enter, a new season.

- What new commitments have I made? For me to honor these commitments, how much time do they require? (i.e., for your emotional healing journey, you need time to decompress after therapy)
- What new commitments are on the horizon? How much time will they require? What new space might you need? (i.e., time to study for the LSAT)
- Where do you feel content and settled? What's contributing to this?

- Where has your tolerance changed (physically and/or mentally)?
- What familiar routines no longer fit your schedule, needs, or interests?
- Where do you feel restless, frustrated, or discontent? What's contributing to this?
- What are you ready to leave behind?
- What new thing do you want to make space for?
- On a scale of one to five, how aligned do you feel to your own definition of purpose and well-being? (Five = very aligned, one = totally misaligned)

Tie It Together:
After answering these questions, I:

Feel: ______________________________
Think: ______________________________
Want to: ______________________________

Socialized to Overoptimize and Perform

Even when we've recognized we're in a new season, honoring that season can be easier said than done. Amid a radically evolving economic and social landscape, we've continued in our pursuit to be the good parents, excellent executives, responsible citizens, and helpful family members we saw so many before us become. Unknowingly, in the process, we've been conditioned to take on so much, for so long, that we think if we're not doing it all and doing it well, we're somehow failing. We're more socialized to overfunction than to attune to our needs, and in this way, we chase the grind, hoping to signal to everyone else (and ourselves) that we're not selfish, indulgent, or falling behind.

This conditioning to *perform* our lives instead of live our lives has us out of sync with life's natural rhythms. We can't catch the beat. We:

- Take on more responsibilities, even when we're already on the verge of burnout
- Continue to travel when we're meant to be home
- Turn down opportunities we've prayed for
- Force relationships that have run their course
- Tell ourselves things like, *You should have learned this skill already*
- Expect aging loved ones to have energy to do what they've always done
- Keep the same schedule even when things around us have changed

When we believe our value and relevance comes from our performance, it's hard to appreciate life's slower, more hidden seasons of investment—the times we're meant to exist behind the scenes and plant seeds for a future harvest. And when we're so used to doing things one way, it's hard to let go of what was and experience a new now.

The battle with ageism and our culture's way of celebrating

production over purpose also means that honoring the seasons of our lives can feel countercultural. As a part of the microwave generation, thanks to technology, we expect things to happen fast. We crave immediate gratification. Our tolerance to wait has decreased, and we've been trained to see incremental progress as an impediment to immediate perfection. In many ways, we have a strained relationship with patience, and it leads us to question the value of life's twists and turns. We're quick to dismiss or rush any season that doesn't feel like a booming success, and we want to banish boring tasks and minimize mundane routines. Sometimes we can be so conditioned to pick up the grind that we don't always honor a season of rest.

Out of Sync: The Quiet Cost of Misalignment

A few months before her birthday, my friend Alex received an unexpected health diagnosis that left her mentally fatigued and logistically burdened. Suddenly, she had weekly doctor's appointments and little time for anything else. It was hard for her to reconcile that, at least for the next few months, her priorities would need to change. One day she called me in frustration.

"Jovi, what am I going to do about my party? I always throw something, but this year I just don't feel like it. You know everyone keeps asking me about my plans. I'm the one who always gets folks together—it's what *I do*! People look forward to it . . . it feels like everyone is waiting on me to plan something, but they don't know what's going on. Maybe I should just plan something small."

My heart broke for my friend; her resistance was only going to add more stress.

Misalignment shows up quietly in our daily choices, the moments we deny ourselves freedom from outdated expectations or deny ourselves the space we need and the help we want. These choices accumulate over time, moments of self-betrayal becoming additional weight we carry on our shoulders. The weight adds up, as many of us are walking around with high blood pressure and low-grade anxiety. This isn't an indictment but an opportunity. It's not a conviction of our failure but a signal that we're not in alignment. When we call out this pattern we can welcome in change. Change we **can** make.

My friend Alex needed permission to pick herself up, even if it meant letting other people down. She needed permission to honor her new season by meeting her new needs. Her life was taking on a new rhythm. Her soft landing came when she stopped trying to do what she'd always done and started receiving the care she now needed.

Honoring the seasons of our lives helps us detach from the misaligned goals and harmful expectations that threaten to eclipse our peace. As our capacity changes, so can our priorities and expectations. When we honor the seasons, we flow into purpose. We respect our present needs, abilities, and limitations. We *live*, not perform, a more honest and abundant life—a life where our intentional behavior and choices support our well-being. This is how we experience a soft landing.

What Keeps Us from Honoring a New Season

At a macro level, because of capitalism and a culture of overconsumption, we see how many of us are conditioned to push through instead of rest, even when the season calls for it. But before we explore how we can better honor our seasons, let's prepare our minds to attune to our behaviors at the micro level. Intrinsic ways of being that without our mindfulness can become threats to our soft landing.

Wired for the Familiar: The Threat of Old Identities and Expectations

Let's start here: As an evolutionary protection, we are neurologically wired to hold on to the past. Our brains use past experiences to anticipate the future, helping us make quick decisions to avoid danger and to prepare for the unknown. But what happens when patterns of the past become harmful to our future? Expectations we once held and things we once believed can become unconscious prisons. Our brains can't always sense the difference between psychological and physiological danger. As such, patterns our brains might cling to can in part be the old identities, and perceptions of success and failure that can become threats to our personal growth and development.

If we've only understood ourselves to be successful or worthy because of one thing, what happens when life unimaginably, and yet, undoubtedly, takes that one thing away? My friend Alex, known for her carefully curated parties and events, cared deeply about her identity of being "the one to throw a fabulous party." When her body made other plans, she struggled to give herself grace in the new season because her identity felt in conflict with her new needs. Alex found her soft landing when she freed herself from the pressures of her identity. She was still someone who could throw a fabulous party, even if the party was for two people instead of two hundred. Just like Alex, our seasons change, and with those changes our capacity shifts. The larger culture that tells us to "push through" and "be who we've always been" leads us to believe that resetting expectations is an act of failure, when in fact, it can be an act of liberation.

Wired for Comfort: The Threat of Grief

New seasons don't just require new logistics or expectations; they ask us to pay attention to our feelings and emotions so we can meet our needs. It's taken me a long time to admit to myself, let alone anyone else, that I may not have a second child. Just the thought of that reality used to bring me to tears. The fear of letting future Jorgie down. The reality of letting present "Me" down. Waves of grief for this dream I didn't know I held so tightly threatened many joyful moments—our impromptu living room concerts, "Family Friday Movie Nights," and sundown neighborhood walks. The emergence of my grief was a signal that I was coming to terms with my life, one that, not just for a season, but a lifetime, didn't include me giving birth to another child. I wanted to avoid the grief that came along with my truth. But once I acknowledged it, I began to find my support—trusted and safe spaces where I could process my journey honestly.

Different emotions come along with seasonal changes, often feelings we want to avoid, like disappointment, jealousy, or regret. These feelings are messy and they don't always have easy explanations or come with comfortable stories. And yet, they're still ours. Psychology gives us the term *experiential avoidance*—the tendency to avoid, or attempt to control or suppress, unwanted internal experiences (including thoughts and emotions). Some feelings are simply *hard* to experience. They squeeze our insides and leave us drained. The inconvenient truth is sometimes we're not prepared to pay the emotional cost of entering into a new season. But as we journey, may we all be given enough fortitude and grace to turn the pages of our story.

Wired to Compare: The Threat of Toxic Comparison

The social comparison theory says we compare ourselves as an innate form of safety and security. It's in part how we understand our social status and self-worth. While there are some benefits to comparison, when taken to unhealthy levels it can become toxic. Toxic comparison is driven by insecurity, fear of failure, or feelings of inadequacy. It is dehumanizing, imprisoning, and how we end up working in careers we never loved or staying in relationships we have outgrown. It's why we take the focus off our winter and give our attention to their summer. All the while forgetting that they had to go through their own winter to get to their version of summer.

Comparison isn't just the thief of joy; it's the primary distraction from our dreams. Not the dreams we think we should have, but the dreams we *know* are tied to our destiny. This dangerous type of comparison distorts our reality, creating in our mind ridiculous timelines for success and isolating us from the help we need.

We can even experience toxic comparison with our *own* past. It's like the times we beat ourselves up for not being able to do something as well as we once did. *I should still be able to run that fast or jump that high.*

We can forget that as adults, we will still take baby steps. Some seasons are for the beginner's pottery class or first time managing a team. These baby steps show up like sloppy first drafts and "silly" mistakes. But in the same way that we wouldn't berate a baby for their wobbly first steps, we shouldn't deny the beauty in our own. It's okay to be frustrated when we know our potential hasn't yet turned kinetic. But we can't let a slow pace make us give up the whole race.

When we feel ourselves slipping into the trap of comparison, we have to audit and change our inputs. Sometimes the people who used to inspire us now incite insecurity, or the friends that once understood our struggle can no longer relate. When this happens, we have to be honest and change our exposure. At times, it's as easy as an unfollow, mute, or delete, at other times, it may require a difficult conversation or distance from a relationship. Remember, these changes don't have to be forever, but just for a season—and maybe not in all ways, but just in one area.

Navigating the Unexpected Seasons

As we've come to experience, at times, without warning, the seasons will change, leaving us breathless and untethered. A divorce. An unexpected bill. Tidal waves of grief slosh onto our new shores of rocky logistics, and we feel like we can't catch our breath. What do we do when we go from child to caregiver? Or from the top of the food chain to the unemployment line? With love, we give ourselves what we need to keep going. We give ourselves the space to be human in the midst of the madness.

We do the next best thing: to love ourselves well. This mantra becomes the entry to our soft landing. We reshuffle schedules, create space for feeling, and refuse to overcommit. We acknowledge that this new season will change us, and so we tether ourselves to things that help our spirits remain intact. We recommit to our loves—our trusted relationships, our faith, and our rituals. We urge ourselves away from isolation and into the arms of community. We lean on lessons from ancestors, and we practice routines that ground us in simple gratitude.

Change that comes without our consent is best handled with our grace. We need to give ourselves grace in our exhaustion, our abilities, and our fear. And importantly, we need grace for our continual evolution. We might not be able to do all that we used to do, but we can still give ourselves the love we deserve.

To truly experience a soft landing, we must let ourselves grieve. Grief is a bridge between seasons. It can walk us into gratitude and carry us to compassion. Our grief reflects our love for something, our appreciation for its existence, and our reverence for its indelible impact on our lives. As we move through the seasons, may we give ourselves permission to miss what was, while over time, preparing for what will be. This can be embodied through experiences like making scrapbooks, taking road trips back home, and sharing memories on phone calls.

We can also prompt healing reflection in and for each other through conversations. Simple questions can help us find the beauty in a past season. For example:

For others:

- What do you learn from that version of you?
- How did living in that city change you?
- What are you taking away from that relationship?

For yourself:

- What did I learn from this person, place, thing, or experience?
- How have I changed?
- What am I proud of and why?

We've built lives we care about, and as things change, we will grieve familiar comforts, voices, people, and places. Our grief changes us, and over time it, too, will evolve. As the seasons move on, may our grief carve out space for renewed peace and daring contentment.

Move in Flow:
How to Find the Rhythm of Each Season

Every Season Has a Purpose

When we honor a season, we respect it. We recognize its presence and acknowledge its value.

During her 2021 acceptance speech at the Emmy Awards, actress Michaela Coel told the audience, "Don't be afraid to disappear." Michaela, known to pull away from the Hollywood spotlight so she can live honestly and create authentically, was getting at a universal truth: There is a time and place for everything.

Some seasons urge us to sow seeds, while others caution us to rest the land. As it is in nature, so it is in our lives. Some seasons ask that we pick things up, while others demand that we put things down. Some require a slower pace, others a limited sprint. Our biggest work might require seasons of isolation and repetitive tasks. Those seasons help us to get away from the noise, so we can get closer to our creativity, closer to ourselves.

And as the seasons change, so do our behaviors. When we're steadying ourselves in a new diet or spiritual discipline, we tend to hibernate, leaning on schedules and limited influences to help us anchor our behaviors. In other seasons, life tells us to sprint to the finish line, so we won't carry any regrets. It's when we find out we only have a few months left with a loved one, so we get on planes, drive to and from doctor's appointments, hold hands while sharing stories, and cook meals around the clock. We know it won't be forever, but it's the truth of that season, and so we give it all we've got.

Seasons come to teach us, prune us, and grow us. But in their messy middle, we don't always understand their value. The toil and sowing of certain seasons can feel like an unwelcome burden, when in fact, even that burden has a purpose. It can help us refine our relationships, sharpen our skills, or deepen our self-trust. The seasons of slowdown prepare us to flourish, and the seasons of hustle prepare us to regenerate our impact.

And just like winter turns into spring, each season comes to an end. A reminder that our human condition is a reflection of what it means to experience sacred release and acceptance. The more we accept that a season has changed, the more we can understand its purpose in our lives.

Honoring each season is about understanding our priorities, assessing our capacity, and managing expectations. It is living with a purpose to honor our needs, gifts, skills, and resources for any given moment, all with the intention to be and live well. Here are three approaches that help us do this well: be clear, be intentional, and be in gratitude.

Be Clear

Let's get clear on what we need. When you slow down, you can notice things more plainly. You can see changes in your body and mental health, and the subtle shifts in your relationships. During this intentional slowdown, you might journal or invite healthy conversations that help you to better understand your feelings, goals, and the help you might need. You can ask yourself questions like:

- What do I need?
- What would help me be well now?
- What has changed around me?
- What is the world asking of me that I am meant to give?
- Where am I pushing where life is asking me to rest?
- What is important to me right now? What is different? What is consistent?
- What are my current core values? How am I living through them?
- What am I uniquely positioned to do in this season?

Once you arrive at a point of clarity, be careful not to judge or dismiss your needs. Your truth doesn't need your judgment—it needs your compassionate response. Here's an example:

> **Need in this season:** My body isn't responding well to running anymore. I need a break and a new workout routine.
> **A soft landing:** I decide to tell my friends, "My body needs a new workout, so I'm going to take a break from running to try Pilates. You're welcome to join me! I'll miss the next few months of running club, but whether

it's at Pilates or not, I still wanna make time to hang out."

Be Intentional

Your intentions reflect your purpose. It's how you lean into the fullness of the present season versus living in the shadows of your past. Instead of life just happening to you, you happen to it. And after taking time to become more clear, you can now make intentional choices to act. This might look like:

- Recognizing you feel distant from your partner, so you suggest a weekly at-home date night
- Noticing you feel lonely, so you begin a virtual book club with friends
- Sensing new independence in your child, so you give them new responsibilities
- Knowing the next two months of work will be particularly stressful, so you create space in your mornings to take a ten-minute meditative walk
- Realizing you've been distracted, so you start a social media fast
- Acknowledging you're bored with your gym routine, so you start a new class with friends
- Reimagining holiday traditions, so you don't just survive the holidays but enjoy them
- Trying a new hobby, so you can discover new interests and joys

- Spending the first ninety days of a new job making a good impression, so you can establish the credibility needed for future impact

My friend Kendra decided to honor her new season of married life by changing her work schedule and getting help with her niece's admissions process. Both things gave her new emotional and physical capacity to focus on her marriage. This was the soft landing she needed.

Your soft landing is in your seasonal permission. For instance: In this season you have permission to stop volunteering at church. (You were on two committees last year; take a break.) Right now you have permission to spend more time at work (you're onboarding new employees; they need you). Respecting the seasons reminds us that at some point, things will inevitably evolve. Perhaps this season will last for a few years, or maybe just a month. But no matter the season, you always have permission to tend to your needs.

Be in Gratitude

Committing to a gratitude practice refines our focus and invites positivity. It might look like a daily prayer of thanks or an evening ritual with a gratitude journal. Ritualizing our gratitude helps us find joy in the present moment. Gratitude ushers in the resilience we need for our hardships and the joy we want for our triumphs. Our gratitude influences our adaptability and how well we accept the impact of every season. Gratitude is undefeated.

I like to think that gratitude concerns itself with every detail of our life. It opens our aperture so we can better see our limitations. It shows us the fresh gifts we can hold because we were brave enough to let something else go. Gratitude helps us find the purpose in it all. It unearths the joy that is hidden beneath pain and grief. And it helps us collect the puzzle pieces of memories that together reflect the breadth and beauty of what we're privileged to experience.

Gratitude will help us laugh again, when for weeks all we have known are tears. Gratitude gives new meaning to old pain and directs our energy, with a knowing anticipation, toward cocreating the mystery of the future. Gratitude reminds us that we have done hard things before and that we can do them again.

We Can Do This

Finding clarity and comfort in a new season takes time, but the benefit to our spirits is undeniable. As a practice, honoring the seasons encourages our gentleness and creates space for our compassion and, ultimately, our soft landing. When hard days come, and it feels like our success is off schedule and our capacity doesn't meet life's demands, I hope we remember all the times we've already reached for alignment instead of pressure. The times we've remembered evolution is a form of grace—a gift that carries us through every day. As we look to honor the seasons of our lives, may we give ourselves the soft landing of alignment instead of the pressure of performance.

An Invitation to Reflect and Act

Give yourself space and time to notice, and then name the season of life you're in:
What would I call this season of my life? ____________
____

Discover this season's priorities:

What is life asking of me?
How do I know?
What am I asking of life?

Use these questions to support your reflection:

What has changed around me?
What has changed within me?
What is my body telling me?

Define your actions:

What can I off-load in this season?
What needs more of my focus and attention?
Given your answers, what changes could you make? Pick one (or more if you'd like).

Think about what your answers mean for your precious resources: energy, time, attention, money, etc.

CHAPTER 5

Appreciate Life's Goodness

"This being human is a guest house. Every morning a new arrival."

RUMI, "THE GUEST HOUSE."

My current voicemail greeting still sounds like the family greeting I recorded when I was eight years old: ". . . And don't forget, life isss wonderful!" Of course, eight-year-old Jovian hadn't had her heart broken yet or lost a job she loved. At eight, my life was wonderful because, as they said in one episode of *Mad Men*, "I had everything. And I had so much of it." But even as I aged and began to experience life's ups and downs, I decided to keep my voicemail the same, only thinking about changing it once. That time? When my husband, George, was admitted to the ICU.

George knew something was off, but nothing was making sense. He was in peak health, having never eaten cleaner or worked out harder. We decided one night that he should just go to urgent care. I stayed home, unsuspecting the worst, and gave a young Jorgie her bath. As I reached for a towel, George called. He gave me the code word we use when something is wrong. He said he was headed to the emergency room. From there, things were a blur of mumbled prayers and my desperate fingers calling others for help. But I do remember getting to the hospital quickly because it was only five minutes away. A fact that I hadn't appreciated much before but suddenly felt like an unearned answer to an unasked prayer. It was grace. It was life's goodness.

You can tell when doctors are concerned but don't want to make you nervous. We had plenty of that. It turns out, George had a massive pulmonary embolism, the kind that kills on the spot. In a swirl, parents were called and surgery was scheduled. My heart raced and my palms got sweaty. I took deep breaths and tried counting the lines on my hands. I smiled at nurses, asked lots of questions, and made small talk, hoping to form enough connection to get the most optimal care. We learned George's surgeon was the best in the country. Wow. There it was again, life's goodness.

After praying with parents preparing to hop on flights and talking to incredible surgeons who infused us with confidence, the procedure was underway. I called one of George's best friends Larry to share an update. The weight of it all brought me to my knees and brought us both to tears. We cried for what felt like forever, and then out of nowhere, Larry said, "That muthaf*cka knows he can't die. He can't leave us here like this!"

Maybe it was because I didn't expect him to say that, or because I was deliriously tired, but I burst out laughing, sliding down the wall as happy tears also slid down my cheeks. The absurdity and truth of what Larry said opened us up. Back and forth we went, laughing and talking about how mad we'd be if George died.

"He expects me to pay off this mortgage by myself?!"

"Who's gonna throw homecoming with me?!"

I'm sure anyone looking at me would've been confused. How did I go from completely swollen with tears to now uncontrollably laughing?

The moments ticked by and Larry and I continued to plead, pray, and advocate for George like crazy. Our time on the phone solidified that someone was with me, and that realization felt *good*. But I knew it wasn't just Larry. Our entire community was showing up and they would help us get through this. My brothers and sister were at home with Jorgie. Brittany was organizing a meal train. Cliff, Amber, Lauren, Louisa, and Ij were sending messages to our other family and friends, and countless others were praying. Later, even more would show up, protecting our house and covering for us at work. They were my goodness. And as in any crisis before, I could lean on them.

My tribe would hold me up and help me land softly, reminding me that even in that moment, life still had goodness.

There Is Still Good

There is so much goodness in this life. The sunray that warms our face at just the right time. The note from a friend telling us that everything is going to be okay. Life's goodness is all around us and within us, calling us to appreciate its perpetual offerings. And often, we do appreciate it. We smile at the person who held the door open for us. We genuinely ask, "How are you?" to the cashier scanning our groceries. Yet, I don't have to tell you, there is so much that makes it hard for us to appreciate life's goodness.

I know for some of us, life has thrown its fair share of body blows. We might have been the casualty of our parents' bad decisions, survivor of ongoing racial injustice, target practice for toxic bosses, or the breeding ground for a rare disease. Through the grief, loss, and disappointment, it's hard to believe that there is still good around us, let alone for us. And when this is our story, I boldly pray that all things good and holy give us enough time to experience a tidal wave of good that will overwhelm the bad.

Because of the hand we've been dealt, for some of us, it's easier to be angry than it is to be joyful. We may have been punished by our past joy or taught that our truth is dangerous. There's a vulnerability to acknowledging the good, an emotional exposure or risk that isn't always comfortable. Not all of us feel at ease "being seen." To be vulnerable to life's goodness is to live—but we're afraid to be caught living, so sometimes we don't; we just perform. This disconnect severs authentic connections, and if we're not careful, we can become too chill, too protected, and too cool to even feel true joy. This is how we begin to dim our light.

Others of us have felt the effects of social media's distortion of reality. We've come to know the external value of documenting our lives to prove that we're living them. We can be so busy capturing the things that signal life is good—snapping photos of beautifully plated meals, curated vacations, and staged re-interactions with our kids—and all the while our food is getting cold and we've forgotten what our child really needed. For some of us, the camera, originally meant to memorialize life's goodness, has stopped us from even experiencing it.

It's hard to appreciate life's goodness if we're moving too quickly to spot it. Too many of us pack our days with so many meetings that we miss the chance to eat a good lunch or to enjoy the good weather outside. It's counterintuitive, but feeling busy can lead us to feeling behind, causing us to work even more. It's hard to see things clearly when we are too busy, too tired, and too overwhelmed to genuinely appreciate them.

Then there are societal obstacles that keep us from seeing life's goodness. It's no secret that capitalism capitalizes on the worst of our tendencies—most of our "entertainment," including the news and reality and scripted TV, highlights fearmongering, envy, and malicious behavior. If this is what we train our eyes to consume for entertainment, we will no doubt experience a distorted aperture when trying to notice the good in the world. Through our large-scale and local media, we're slowly training each other not to see, or believe, that good still exists.

But life's goodness is all around us, if only we could slow down just enough to see it. We must sharpen what I call our "joy eyes." Joy eyes are trained to look for life's goodness. They see the goodness in the friend who calls at just the right time, the disarming stranger who shares your smile in the elevator, and the surprising confidence you find in driving to a destination without GPS. The perfect song that comes on at *just* the right time? Life's goodness. A hug from someone you love? Life's goodness. The forgiveness you receive after you've caused harm? Life's undeniable goodness. Goodness can be the cookout plate that makes you two-step, finding a dollar bill on the sidewalk, or watching three generations of a family reunite at the airport. Everything changes when we attune ourselves to the good that's all around us.

To appreciate life's goodness is to bear witness to its magic with all your available senses. It's not only seeing life's goodness, but daring to hear, taste, smell, and touch it. When we appreciate life's goodness, we bring it close and let its power penetrate our tender places. It's a vulnerable act, as it urges us, at least temporarily, to let go of cynicism and fear, the things that so often harden our hearts. But through this appreciation, we let our hearts be softened, ready then to expand. In that expansion, we can collect more goodness, and our hearts grow stronger, able to pump out more of that goodness into the world. In all of this, we pad our hearts, giving them extra capacity to heal from life's inevitable heartbreaks. This padding gives us a soft landing, the kind I want to invite you to cocreate today and every day.

A Self-Reinforcing Cycle

In an article for the Northeast Georgia Physicians Group, Dr. Hannah Packiam refers to negative thoughts as ANTs (automatic negative thoughts). I love this analogy! Just one won't ruin the picnic, she says, but if left unaddressed, more will come and quickly ruin a good thing.

What we focus on amplifies. That's why if we focus on the bad, that's likely what we'll see. As we've explored in other chapters, there is a neuroscientific component to how we can land softly. Our brains have a reticular activating system (RAS), or what we could think of as a search engine. This RAS filters out various pieces of information based on our thoughts, aka what we tell it to search for. And because our bodies have been evolutionarily designed to protect and save our energy, our brains will sort out information that doesn't align with our thoughts. For instance, if we say, "Today is going to be a bad day!," we will ignore the glowing remarks from our boss and focus on the bad weather outside or the pothole we accidentally drove over. Psychologically speaking, it's confirmation bias—our brain's desire to confirm our thoughts so it can keep us comfortable and "safe."

Thankfully, we can use these phenomena for good! Through neuroplasticity, our brain's ability to change, we can train our brains to notice the good all around us. Every time we notice the good, we are reinforcing a habit of hope, digging new, deeper neural pathways in our brains. The more we notice the good around us, the easier and more automatic it becomes over time. This is incredibly powerful as we think about how we can support our mental health, especially when we go through hard times. Being open to noticing life's goodness is a power move. It can help us rewire our thinking, lower our anxiety, and fight against depression. And while we may still need clinical support and at times medications from our doctors, appreciating life's goodness can help us combat the negative ants that are threatening to hijack our picnic.

Something incredible happens when we allow ourselves to notice life's goodness around us. Eventually, we start to expect it. We begin to believe that goodness is always possible, even on the hardest days. In other words, we find our way back to hope.

And hope? Hope is our lifeline. Along with love, it is our most formidable weapon against everything that would tell us that we should give up. In appreciating life's simple goodness, we let hope whisper, *Something else is coming*. Even on our hard days, hope helps us realize we can find strength to do the next best thing: We can drink a glass of water. We can go for a walk. We can call our people. We can return to therapy or go back to AA. When we appreciate life's goodness, we reconnect with the power of hope.

Larry's words reminded me that I would laugh again, and throughout George's recovery I held on to the goodness of that laugh. Later I would sit in that hospital room, being struck by the dichotomy of life. I thought, *This could be one of the worst days of my life. And at the same time, there is someone, somewhere, who's literally having the best day ever.*

Isn't that something? How strange and perfectly like life. Even during our hard times, someone else is still experiencing something else that is so good.

Ways We Appreciate Life's Goodness

It can feel overwhelming and at times completely daunting to find our way back to hope. But as it is with many things, it's the small things that we do over time that make the biggest difference. We have to stack our days with the good stuff, each day noticing and appreciating just a little bit more of life's goodness. This is an act of defiance during a time when we're inundated with bad news on purpose and working against a larger system that is betting that we'll fall into apathy and become slaves to despair. But it's in our small, intentional, and consistent ways of remembering life's goodness that we find our relief and soft landing.

Collect Joy Points

There are pain points, and then there are what I like to call Joy Points. Joy Points are moments that make our souls smile. The more Joy Points we collect, the more joyful we feel. And over time, because of our brain's neuroplasticity, the more we notice, or collect, Joy Points, the more we begin to understand just how worthy we are to experience life's goodness—a true soft landing.

As you go about your day, pay close attention to the small but mighty things that lift your spirit. Write them down in a journal or in your notes app. Collect screenshots of encouraging texts from friends and save complimentary emails from coworkers in a special folder (mine is called "Don't forget this"). Joy Points can be high fives with strangers at a game or funny stories from family. They don't always have to be life-changing, just life-affirming. The more we collect Joy Points, the more we have in reserve during tough times, the days we need them most. On our hardest days, each Joy Point is a breadcrumb back to hope.

Slow Down

When I think of good things, I often think of the Bible's creation story. In this story, over seven days, God created the heavens, the earth, and all that dwelt within it. Throughout that week, the Bible says that God saw that it was good. But on the seventh day, God rested from all the hard and good work that had been done.

The divine lesson in this? If God slowed down long enough to name and notice the good, so can we. I assume God could have done it all with a supernatural finger snap (does God have fingers?), but God recognized the value of an intentionally slower pace, a pace that allowed God to (1) rest and (2) appreciate the good.

If you want to take good care of yourself, you have to slow down. If you want to appreciate life's goodness, you must change your pace to witness the good in action. This could look like decompressing your schedule, inviting spaciousness on your weekends, or practicing active listening in conversations so you can hear the heart behind the words being said. What other good could we experience if we just slowed down?

Here's a simple invitation for you: The next time you hear a baby giggle, don't rush away. Slow down and soak it up!

Reset Your Boundaries

Too many people have access to us. From strangers on the internet to coworkers emailing at 9:13 p.m., the flow of chaotic energy on top of regularly scheduled adulting (aka constant decision-making) can run us ragged. We only have capacity for so much. Our spirits are precious containers (I think of mine as a rose gold glass) that can be easily overwhelmed with negative behavior disguised as breaking news or entertainment, and relationships that have turned toxic.

As much as we try to control our social media feeds, the algorithm undoubtedly will change without our permission, and sometimes (okay, most times) the news or the group chat are bringing you more angst than relief. Let's be clear: It's not that these spaces can't *also* harvest the good we can appreciate. But it is our job to discern when that's happening, and when it's not.

To better appreciate life's goodness, you might need to put new gates around your relationships, the one with technology included. Here are some things to try with technology:

- Spend the first thirty minutes of your morning without technology (set your intentions before the news sets them for you!)
- Put your phone on DND after 9 p.m. (wind down at your own pace)
- Decide when and how often you'll use social media
- Try my friend Morgan's "post and ghost" (post your content and then close the app)
- Limit notifications from critical apps
- Update your news hygiene (determine the news outlets or key voices you trust and go to them intentionally versus scrolling through the chaos)

Working with a therapist and/or a coach might give you the additional support you need when resetting your boundaries. When we protect ourselves from unnecessary negative inputs, we ensure we have the energy and mental capacity to receive the good around us.

Wednesday Wins

For about a decade, one of my friend groups, lovingly called the "Ain't Shit Crew" (ironically, we're all very much about our business—spiritually, physically, and emotionally), has practiced what we call Wednesday Wins. Winsday, if you will! Every Wednesday, we share a Joy Point. The type of win doesn't matter—finding a new hairdresser or getting a job promotion, we celebrate them all. This ritual has helped us to notice, appreciate, and embrace the good stuff in our lives even more. This is especially powerful, as we're all Black Women reminding each other, in a world that says otherwise, that we deserve good things in this life. It's also helped us practice celebrating each other. As with anything, the more you practice, the more fluent and comfortable you will be, especially in high-stakes moments. Even in a tough season, it is easier to still appreciate life's goodness after consistently practicing a ritual like Wednesday Wins. After a while, you begin to see how all our wins matter.

What's your version of Wednesday Wins? Maybe you start a joy chat with your family. The topic: What's bringing you joy today? Maybe you start a gratitude train with friends. The possibilities are endless!

We Are Good

We can be soft landings.

As we begin to appreciate life's generous offerings, we are

changed on a molecular level. The more we notice the good, the more we will believe that there *is* good, align ourselves *with* good, and treat ourselves and others *as* good. The power of this choice is exponential. This practice fortifies the work we do in our local communities and the policies we advocate for globally. It brings immeasurable value to how we perceive the world and ourselves within it. It reminds us that we can be each other's soft landings.

Everywhere we look, there are opportunities to witness the multiplying effect of appreciating life's goodness. With an act of creativity, we can inspire a new artist or entrepreneur. And with an act of bravery, we can enlist an army for justice. This soft landing has a reverberating impact on our souls and those we touch. The more that I give myself the soft landing of appreciating life's goodness, the more you'll do it, too. A simple act of gratitude can travel around the world. We open one door with a smile, and the next person thinks they should, too, then the next, and the next . . .

And someone, somewhere, thinks to themselves, "Wow, life is wonderful."

An Invitation to Reflect and Act

There are good things all around you. You, yourself, are one of those good things. Let's take a second and appreciate you and all of life's goodness. Then let's think about who we can share it with.

How do I bring goodness into my community? In my family?

What do I appreciate about myself?

I am grateful for ___________________________________.

I have been gifted __________________________________.

What's one good thing I can share with someone I love?

____.

How has life surprised you?

Part II

Soft Landings for Hard Days

When We Long to Be Gentle

Sit with me.

Life is chaotic. What we want to do isn't always what we choose to do. And what we dream of doing isn't always what we can manage in the moment. During these times, we're often hard on ourselves, pushing our bodies toward burnout and denying ourselves self-compassion and gentleness.

On these days, we could use some help finding a soft landing. So curl up, sprawl out, or squat down (toilet reads are my favorite) and read on.

SOFT LANDING #1

For the day it's hard to ask for help

You were never meant to do it all alone

You pull your car into the garage and sit there until you hear *click*, a signal that the door is closed and you've just clocked into your second job.

Any minute the after-school bus will drop off the kids.

You look at your watch, silently soaking up every second of silence before you're called to command a choir of chaos.

Your body is tired after a long day of work, but you know there is even more work to be done once you step inside. Your partner won't be home till later, so it's just you. You're not wearing any sleeves, but you still pretend to roll them up, mentally preparing to handle all that's on your plate. Your to-do list scrolls like a ticker tape across your mind:

Cook dinner; lead the school's fundraising meeting; Instacart groceries for Mom; send updates for the family reunion; schedule doctor's appointments. . . .

The list goes on.

You begin to sink into your seat, each responsibility weighing heavily on your shoulders. You have quick thoughts about asking for help but rationalize each one away. You think, *I don't want to burden anyone else. . . . I agreed to this. . . . They won't do it as well as I would. . . . I'm my mother's child. . . . I should be able to handle this. . . . By the time I tell Mike, I could have just done it myself.*

But you're tired of doing it all.

You've been here before, though this time, something is urging you to think again. Something is saying that it doesn't have to be this way, that you don't have to do it all by yourself. You desperately want that voice to be right, but you're not sure anyone would help, that they'd still see you underneath all that you do.

I know it hurts to think that you can't be held in your time of need. That you have to be the one to carry it all. You're tired, and some days—really, most days—the load is just too much. Sure, you can admit that you *did* ask for this life, but that doesn't mean you didn't want help living it. So why does it feel like asking for help is like waving a dangerous white flag? Like with one wave, someone will take it all away from you. Or with one ask for help, you're suddenly a burden, and somehow inferior or a failure.

And there they are—the fears that keep you going, that keep you believing you must do it all alone.

But what if those fears are lying to you? What if there's another way?

What if:

You're not a failure because you want help.

You're not lazy because you don't want to do it alone.

You're no less capable or grateful because you want support.

What if:

You are worthy to be helped.
Your discernment will find the right help.
Your helpers are nearby, ready and willing to help you.

The world wants you to believe that asking for help is a toxic trait, when not asking for help is the thing that could kill you. Don't let this weight take you down.

You're not weak because you don't want to keep holding it all. It was too much to carry in the first place. No matter how long you have trained for "this" or how strong you are, your back wasn't meant to carry so much for so long. In this season, your strength is in your wisdom. This wisdom is as much a shield as it is an ancestral sage telling you to *let them help you.*

You're tempted to believe these words, to, in your mind, let them click in place like that garage door. You can see that they have truth, that they can help you imagine a world where you share your load.

But you're still trying to figure out if the weight of potential disappointment is heavier than the load you already carry.

I get it; that concern is real.

But go with me here. What if people won't let you down this time? What if they'll actually pick you up? Imagine what you could do, how you would feel!

And okay, what happens if they *do* let you down? You do what you've always done when things happen that you can't control. You pick up the pieces and try again. You take one small step after another. You learn who you can trust and who needs more guidance. You prepare for people to do it their own way and not exactly like you would do it. You consider maybe getting it done is more important than getting it done your way. Especially if it means you can carry a little less.

When you feel the urge to push through on your own, I want you to turn down any whispers of shame that want you isolated and weary under your tattered superhero cape. Instead, I want you to turn up the confident voice of your inner guide—the love inside of you that is saying, *I am worthy to be held*.

You have done enough. And just because you *can* do it alone does not mean you *should* do it alone. There is power in your ask—a power that affirms your helpers and frees your soul.

Today, when it feels hard to ask for help and easier to do it all alone, let your gentle hands put down your load and receive some care.

Daily Invitations

An invitation to affirm

As you make your way through this day, hold these affirmations close to your head and heart:

I am worthy to be helped.

I am worthy to be seen.
I have people in my life who will help me.

An invitation to reflect

What is stopping you from asking for help?
What would good help look like?
What do you need?
Where could you find good support?
What are you willing to try?

An invitation to commit

From today's soft landing:

The lesson I will take is ______________________________.
The commitment I will make is ________________________.

SOFT LANDING #2

For the day you're afraid of the outcome

You are surrounded by love

It was only a few days into 2023 when I got a call from my doctor urging me to return to the Breast Health Services for a follow-up visit regarding my left breast. This same left breast had already undergone numerous mammograms, ultrasounds, and two biostatic biopsies, plus, on the positive side, fifteen months of breastfeeding. A million thoughts vied for my attention, but they all brought me back to one question: Will I have to tell my daughter the same news my mother had once told me?

"I have breast cancer."

I sat in the waiting room feverishly counting floor tiles, begging myself to stay calm. I'll never forget how hard my left knee was shaking, and how painful it felt to have my makeup-filled tears burn my eyes, tears I was too frozen with fear to wipe away. All I could do was pray.

> *Creator, you know me better than I know myself. You know what concerns me. You know what worries me. You know what ails me. You know, intimately, the way forward. So I boldly ask: Will you go with me? Will you walk with me into the unknown? I pray that the strength of my ancestors, loved ones, and your awesome Spirit will cover every inch of my body as I make my way forward.*
>
> *I am afraid, and I am unsure. I am begging you to remind me that you are bigger than my fears. Right now, when I am afraid, I need you to remind me that your love for me encompasses every worry and every disappointment.*
>
> *I sit in gratitude knowing that you care about me and that you hear my prayer. I sit in gratitude knowing that you are around every corner. I sit in gratitude knowing that you see me.*

How do we learn to wait well? The waiting room is an excruciating place, and it will come for us all. I wonder what waiting room you are in right now. Maybe you're waiting for the phone call to say if you got the job or lost it. Or if your new nephew has arrived. Or if the unimaginable has happened. I bet you're holding on with everything you've got, doing your best while you wait, remembering to breathe and sipping water as you can. My waiting room prayer represents what we most want when we're afraid and staring into the unknown: the promise that someone will walk with us, no matter what's on the other side. In our waiting, when we're scared shitless, sweating uncontrollably, or overwhelmed with competing emotions, we can find a soft landing by confronting the lies that fear likes to tell us:

> That we are alone in our pain.
> That no one has ever felt like we do.
> That we won't make it.
> That the worst-case scenario is going to happen.
> That you don't have enough to get through this.

And then there's love.

Love reminds us we were created in love and are surrounded by love. Love reminds us that generations past, present, and future have stood where we stand, no matter how different the terrain.

Love reminds us that someone has been in your shoes and has a story to tell. Love reminds us that we won't have to face the worst-case scenario alone. Love reminds us that it may turn out better than we could have imagined.

Love reminds us that love is enough. While we wait together, remember that you are, in this moment and every moment after it, covered in a love that transcends circumstance. Tap into your most intrinsic, most innate knowing, that intuitive voice that whispers, *You are loved, and you are not alone.*

You are surrounded by the evidence of this truth. As you look outside, you are warmed by the same loving sun that grants heat and nourishment to a stranger thousands of miles away. The trees you forget to acknowledge still speak your name as they offer you oxygen and shade. You can call forth the memory of people who have held your hand, rubbed your back, and are ready to do it again.

Today, I want you to land softly, remembering that you are not alone, and that you are so very loved.

Daily Invitations

An invitation to affirm

As you make your way through this day, hold these affirmations close to your head and heart:

I am surrounded by love.
I can't control the outcome, but I can control my response.
I will always have choices to make.
No matter what's up ahead, I will not walk the road alone.
Write your own: ________________________________

An invitation to reflect

What are you feeling in this moment?
What do you need?
What support would feel good?
What choices can you make today?

An invitation to commit

From today's soft landing:

The lesson I will take is ______________________________.

The commitment I will make is _________________________.

SOFT LANDING #3

For the day you're pushing yourself too hard

Not every day requires everything

You had big plans for the day. You were going to hit the gym in the morning, prepare for a big team meeting, and even make your own lunch. Not to mention, you planned to finish two pitch decks and some overdue chores. This was the plan, but nothing's working out. You woke up tired, logging barely three hours of rest thanks to night sweats. But instead of adjusting today's plans, you try to push through.

By midmorning you're exhausted, frustrated, and annoyed with everything and everyone.

In the midst of everything it may be hard to remember, but: *Every day doesn't require everything.* It's hard for us to grasp we're still holding on to old expectations. Your full slate of plans was betting on a full night's sleep. But instead of coming to terms with your exhaustion, you're holding on to what you planned—and holding yourself to a standard that only sets you up for disappointment.

On days like today, you're tempted to be hard on yourself, feeling guilty for what you can't do or won't accomplish. If your old expectations begin to create a new disappointment, you can begin to question what seemed sure and rational, like your worthiness and rest.

You worry that you'll fall too far behind and so you think you need to give today more than what you actually have to give.

Okay friend, hear me out. What if you *are* giving it all you've got. And today's "all" just looks a bit different. What if it's the best you've got for today? The truth is our best varies based on our circumstances.

And what if today doesn't require everything, anyway?

What if, instead of entertaining guilt, you spent your energy rightsizing the day's expectations to meet your honest capacity? This is how you can be gentle with yourself. This is how you honor your humanity.

Try to remember this: *You don't need to use your extraordinary strength on a very ordinary day.*

I'm curious, *What is today asking of you?*

Today might be asking for some of your protection. So how do you protect yourself from yourself? How do you handle days when you ask more from yourself than you have to give? How do you handle the inevitable disappointment?

We distinguish the voices that are in our heads. We decide what voice we need to turn up, turn down, or mute altogether. Asking ourselves:

What is our inner parent saying?

What does our inner child need?

What does our inner adult advocate for?

To ease into this soft landing, start to turn down whatever voice is connected to an unworthy fear. Fear of not being a good enough partner, sibling, friend, or employee. A fear that, if we don't push ourselves, today's a failure and so are we.

When we feel this fear, and this pressure, we are invited to remember that we are in charge of how we respond to what the day brings. We have permission to release old expectations. We've committed to our well being, and so we can pivot out of respect for that promise. We can say to ourselves, *You know when you need to change your mind. I trust you to keep me safe.*

You don't have to push through it; you can be gentle with yourself. Today, releasing old expectations isn't an indictment that you're starting to expect less of yourself. It's a sign that you're starting to protect yourself even more.

Daily Invitations

An invitation to affirm

As you make your way through this day, hold these affirmations close to your head and heart:

I don't need to use my extraordinary strength on my ordinary days.

Loving my body is good stewardship.

Changing my plans can be a responsible choice.

Write your own: ________________________________

An invitation to reflect

What am I expecting out of myself today?

What is truly needed of me today?

How can I be more kind to myself?

What new boundary can I create with my wellbeing in mind? (For example: *No chores after 8 p.m.*)

An invitation to commit

From today's soft landing:

The lesson I will take is ________________________.

The commitment I will make is ____________________.

SOFT LANDING #4

For the day you need permission to rest

Your rest is nonnegotiable

You don't have to do this. You don't have to keep going and going, like a bunny with a battery strapped to their back. You don't have to pretend you have more to give than you do. You don't have to live running on *E*. I know why you turned to this page, so I'm not going to wait to tell you what you need to hear: **You can rest now.**

You have done so much, for so many, and for so long. But I know you're afraid to admit that you're this tired. To you, the exhaustion feels like a guilty verdict. But I promise it's not. What if I told you that you're tired because of a larger issue? What if I told you that you're not the only one?

So many of us are holding on for dear life, when we should be resting, enjoying, and nurturing what *is* our dear life. Of course, we're meant to create things, spend time with people, build and do meaningful work. But that doesn't mean we have to live beyond ourselves every single day. But you know that. Which, again, is why you're here. So I'm going to gently remind you: *You have permission to rest.*

Life may not be as chaotic as much as it's become a perpetual grind, in this season at least. Always something to do, fix, solve, provide, and thankfully even enjoy. Baby showers, trips with friends, community engagements, etc. There's a lot you're trying to honor and take care of. You're trying to be a good sibling, daughter, son, parent, friend, employee, citizen, community member. . . . fill in the blank. Yes, that, too.

You're wondering if you've done enough to rest. And the answer is **yes**. But it's not the long list of things you've done that makes you a candidate for rest. It's the fact that you're human and you must rest. I once read, "If your body whispers for a break, don't wait for the scream." Listen to what your body is telling you. It's not lying to you. Is your body screaming?

As adults, we're sometimes like newborn babies who don't know how to rest. When she was first born, like most babies, my daughter, Jorgie, struggled to sleep. After the first few weeks, my husband, George, completely exhausted, looked at me through withered eyes and asked, "If she's so tired, why doesn't she just go to sleep?" Through my own barely opened eyes I replied, "Because she doesn't know how."

Friend, you're not alone in your exhaustion. When we have days like today, we're reminded that some of our hardest work is learning to rest. Confronting our desire to prove by doing.

I know sometimes it feels like if you rest, you'll fall behind or miss something you needed to do. And so you think it's better to just skip the rest and plan ahead. It's hard to believe that your rest isn't a hazard to your success. That it's not a drain to your dreams or an existential threat to your progress. But we've learned from the Nap Bishop, Tricia Hersey, that our rest is resistance. It's necessary in a world that reserves grace and rest for those in power and leaves the rest of us to think, *We have to earn a good night's sleep.*

Today, I'm giving you permission to rest. But more days like this will come, and you've got to give that permission to yourself, urgently. You can't depend on slow-changing systems to honor your sacred humanity. You have to prioritize the somatic healing work of re-regulating your nervous system with breathwork, mindfulness, and healthy movement. You deserve that. You need that.

You have to say to yourself, *Any feeling that I am unworthy of rest is the antithesis to my existence. I was born worthy of every good and perfect thing that my Creator has endowed me with, and that includes rest.*

Today, you have eternal permission to swaddle yourself in comfort and compassion. You have permission to rest into the life that you want. I know resting often feels scary, like you'll miss something if you stop doing and just let yourself be. But think about what you miss if you *don't* close your eyes. If you don't take time to daydream. What dreams won't you see? What restoration will you miss?

Today, your path to rest reminds you to see the difference between some eternal truths and some systemic lies.

Systemic lies:

Rest is lazy, wasteful, and indulgent.
We can work our way to worthiness.
Our value comes from what we do.
Our responsibilities demand our perfection, leaving us no time to rest.

Eternal truths:

Rest is productive, wise, and sacred.
You are worthy while you rest.
You are more than what you produce.
Our responsibilities don't strip us of our humanity; they expand it.

Just know every time you choose to rest, whether you're in bed or casually staring at the wall letting daydreams flow like movie trailers, you are tending to your humanity. Your rest is restorative. Your rest is so much, but at the core, it's how you remind yourself how worthy you are.

You deserve you. So promise me you won't run past yourself, okay?

I'll talk to you later. Enjoy your rest. ☺

Daily Invitations

An invitation to affirm

As you make your way through this day, hold these affirmations close to your head and heart:

Rest isn't a nice-to-have; it's a must-have.
I'm too divine to refuse my call to rest.
I'm more than what I produce.
Rest is renewal.
Write your own: ________________________________

An invitation to reflect

What is your relationship with rest?
How does that story support you in living well?
What new story might you need to tell yourself?
Who needs to hear your new story?
What happens to your body when you don't rest?
What does good rest look like for you?

An invitation to commit

From today's soft landing:

The lesson I will take is ________________________.
The commitment I will make is ____________________.

SOFT LANDING #5

For the day you're afraid to change

Don't let a "what if" turn into a "why didn't I?"

Michelle has notoriously luscious curls. The kind that move on beat. Even still, she felt like she wanted to have a new look. She called her friend Keia for advice.

Michelle: "*Soooo, I'm thinking about going for a bob. What do you think? A straight blunt cut right below my chin.*"
Keia: "*Oooo snap, that's gonna be so fly on you! Do it!*"
Michelle: "*I know right?! Ughhh, I dunno though.*"
Keia: "*Wait, why not? What's wrong?*"
Michelle: "*. . . Well, what if I love it?*"
Keia: "*. . . And that's a bad thing?*"
Michelle: "*No, not completely. But what if I love it so much that I don't want my curls anymore?*"

Keia: *"Girl, please. Your curls are too great not to love. You can have different looks for different decades. Also, I'm pretty sure it's okay if you love a new thing."*
Michelle: *"But what if I can't afford to keep it up?"*
Keia: *"Michelle, stop. You're talking yourself out of something you want to do. You can have a new look! You don't have to stay the same person. You're allowed to change, babe."*

Sometimes, we're all like Michelle. Afraid to change careers, afraid to move to new cities, afraid to leave relationships. And understandably so; change can be hard. It asks you to let go. And it makes you contend with the unknown. And boy, is that unknown scary. This is what makes days like today, when you're afraid to change, so uncomfortable. In your fear of the unknown, your "what ifs" are rarely positive. The scenarios you ping-pong back and forth don't always include the best-case scenario. It feels like one wrong move and you won't be able to recover. How do you know if you're making the right decision? Should you just stay where you are? Hold on to the relationship? Decline the offer?

I'm thinking about you today, and I want to remind you to be gentle with yourself as you consider a possible change. Let me ask you: Are you worrying right now, or are you planning with your dreams in mind?

My friend Callan once said to me, "You know, Jovi, worry isn't advanced planning." And she's right. Worry robs us of our peace and makes us waste time on things that may never come true. Our fears often deny our dreams entry into reality.

Today, when you're afraid to change but know that you should, you can decide that fear doesn't get to make your decisions. Remember this: Fear extinguishes the flames of your dreams, whereas hope gives them oxygen. So take your time finding your way to hope. Connect with the community that will hype you up, and the mentors and friends that will show you that change is possible. Let yourself dream, remembering to leave space for grace in your "what ifs."

Before you know it, you'll look up and love who you've become. Knowing all along, whatever your choice, grace has helped you make it beautiful.

Daily Invitations

An invitation to affirm

I am worthy of my dreams.
I am worthy of my best-case scenario.
My best-case scenario can become reality.
I will decide from hope, not fear.
Write your own: ____________________

An invitation to reflect

What are you afraid of and why?
What is the story you're telling yourself?
What do you need?
What would it look like to decide out of hope? Out of fear?

An invitation to commit

From today's soft landing:

The lesson I will take is ______________________________.

The commitment I will make is _______________________.

When We Need to Feel Our Feelings

Sit with me.

It's easy to talk ourselves out of feeling what we're feeling. We can judge our emotions to the point that we want to hide them from ourselves. On these days, when we're ashamed of how we truly feel, we need to escape to a soft landing that has room for our inconvenient emotions. A place that offers us honest reflection and connection. Land softly with me as we step into some messy, yet very familiar, hard days.

SOFT LANDING #6

For the day you feel left out

Sometimes we're left out, and sometimes we're pulled out

A quick scroll through your timeline lets you confirm what you already suspected. Yep, everyone's there but you. You wondered why the group chat had been so quiet. *I guess they don't need to chat when they're all together. Did I miss my invitation? Should I've asked to go? Maybe they thought I was too busy. Maybe it wasn't intentional. Maybe it was.*

Your rational and irrational thoughts swirl as your true feelings come to the surface. You feel left out. And you hate how bad this feels. The sudden weight in your stomach and your sweaty palms, serving you notice that you're wounded. Reality is too obvious to ignore. Intentional or not, you've been left out, and now you feel crushed.

The world tells you it's immature to admit that this hurts—that you feel small. Your chest tightens at the realization, a crushing understanding forming quickly in your mind. They didn't want you there. And just like that, oh, how insignificant you feel . . . again. You are instantly back in your fourteen-year-old skin, struggling to make sense of the world around you and wondering why, on Monday, they wanted to sit with you, and now, today, they don't. Today, it feels like you're the big kid who is still trying to make it right for the little kid inside you who got left out, picked last, bullied, and overlooked. The wound you thought you healed by moving thousands of miles away, and with your promotions and new friends, is suddenly exposed. It feels as raw and tender as the first time.

The trap of getting older is the misplaced expectations we put on our feelings, as if they have an expiration date. It feels especially true today, when just admitting how insignificant, insecure, mistaken, angry, and disappointed you feel seems like a failure on your part. You're probably saying to yourself, *Why do I even care? We're not in grade school anymore.* As if that was the only acceptable time to feel this way. And this is when it feels especially hard to stop this feeling from becoming a personal indictment or damning blow to your self-esteem.

It's okay to admit that you want to be included. That you liked knowing that they'd chosen you, just like you'd chosen them. And now, for whatever reason, it's clear that's changed, even if there was no malicious intent. In this new reality, one where you're on the outside, even for just a short while, you'll have to find your way forward. On a day like today, FOMO might just be the cute bag you carry to hide your true feelings: the shock, disappointment, and even betrayal. Calling it FOMO is how you dilute the pain; after all, it's much easier to say you have FOMO than to spell out your feelings: *I feel overlooked. I feel lonely.*

When you're ready to find your soft landing, you'll have to let yourself feel your way through the pain. Even if at first you only whisper it to yourself, you are another step closer to landing softly. So go ahead and whisper it. I'll sit here with you.

I know you're looking for wisdom, a perspective that's helped others through this. Wisdom says it hurts today, and it'll probably still hurt tomorrow, and even the day after. But every day is another step toward your healing.

It's tempting to turtle or ostrich, to make yourself invisible as an act of self-preservation. Still, I wonder if today, somehow, you can return to yourself with a love that says, *I will still be seen.* There's something to be said about radically including your full self while healing from the pain of exclusion. This is how you escape to grace.

You can't choose how they hurt you, but you can choose how you want to heal. You may find relief in rationalizing the facts. You think through the objective truths. Other times, you might need to assume a positive purpose from the pain. Like, maybe instead of being left out, God is pulling you out. Maybe this was bound to happen and only a matter of time before you made your escape. Maybe their actions were inexcusable, but intent forgivable. Maybe you'll choose to reconcile. Maybe, maybe, maybe. Right now, you're not so sure, and neither am I. But at the right time, it will *all* become clear.

And in the meantime, give yourself space to feel and time to heal.

Daily Invitations

Invitation to affirm

There is a way forward.
I am learning from this experience.
I'm a good person worthy of healthy relationships.
Write your own: ______________________________

Invitation to reflect

What can I learn from this?
What would I do differently, if anything?
What has this experience made space for?
What do I still believe about myself?
Who else in my trusted care circle do I need to process this with? (e.g., my therapist, my coach, another friend)

Invitation to commit

From today's soft landing:

The lesson I will take is ______________________.
The commitment I will make is ___________________.

SOFT LANDING #7

For the day you want to celebrate but have no one to call

Just because you want them to hold the space, doesn't mean that they can

You used to call them when you got good news, but now you hesitate. Are we talking about this enough? How disheartening it feels to lose your places of celebration. Not the physical spaces, but the people who once held your joy. Something changed and you don't know when it was. Or maybe it's been like this and you just didn't realize it. Maybe you've always had different love languages. Whatever it is, something's different. Today's a perfect example. You have great news to share, and you want to share it with your people. Well, you *think* they're your people, but something inside you, something you can't ignore, is telling you to put down the phone. The last time you told them some good news, you *thinnnnkk* they said, "I'm proud of you"? Or maybe offered a half-hearted, "I knew you could do it."

You don't remember exactly what they said, but you do remember how it made you feel. It felt more performative than honest. More trite than loving. And that's not something you're willing to ignore.

You're trying to make sure that you aren't ascribing blame where you shouldn't. I know you're thinking, maybe I should've considered their feelings before I shared my news. Maybe they just had a bad day. Or friend, maybe what you're sensing is right: They can't handle your good news. This possibility is tough to swallow. And I know it feels unnerving, sad, and disappointing.

This might *not* be a surprise for you, which, perhaps, makes this feel even worse. You knew something was changing. They weren't returning calls. They seemed to be less interested in your life, even though you've always been interested in theirs. The harsh reality of complicated relationships in misaligned seasons. The truth is settling in: *Right now, they can't be who you want them to be*. But you still wish they could be.

I don't know when, but let's trust that in time, you'll release that expectation. Today, take the space you need to discover your feelings so you can find a way to heal.

Let's not forget why you wanted to call in the first place. You have something to celebrate! You're worthy of celebrating, whether they can do it with you or not. This moment, this achievement, this milestone, whatever it is, it's a blessing and it counts! Let's take a moment and be grateful.

You should celebrate this! You can write yourself a note and affirm that you've been given a great gift. Celebrating is a way of saying, "Thank you." Every time we do this, it's like the Universe whispers back, *I trust you with joy.* In all of this, we understand just how fleeting life is and how quickly things can turn from bad to good and vice versa.

I know today's been tough. Some soft landings come with hard truths. Like, sometimes, the person we want to call is no longer the person we *should* call. Our desire for them to hold the space won't always create their capacity to do so. You might want to call your mom, but maybe your coworker is the better person to celebrate with. And just maybe this win is too big for the group chat's flimsy likes and hearts. Perhaps you take this to God first and let the Universe sort out the details later.

I know this experience is difficult, and you're unsure if you have who you need. But I hope these words feel good: Congratulations! I am so, so happy for you!

Daily Invitations

Invitation to affirm

I am worthy of celebrating!
I am standing in the middle of my answered prayer.
I won't let my good things pass me by.
I will discover new people to celebrate with me.
I will celebrate myself.
I am so proud *of myself.*
Write your own: ____________________________

Invitation to reflect

What does celebrating mean to me?
How do I want to feel?
How do I want to be encouraged? Supported?
Who (if anyone) might I need to speak with?

Invitation to commit

From today's soft landing:

The lesson I will take is ____________________________.
The commitment I will make is ________________________.

SOFT LANDING #8

For the day you realize your parents are human, too

We thought they knew it all, but they never did

For his seventy-fourth birthday, my dad traveled to Mongolia for an outdoor excursion of a lifetime—sleeping in tents, taking hours-long horseback treks, and slurping fresh spring water from cupped hands, the whole shebang. I was equal parts thrilled for him and terrified for me. My dad, to his core, is a deeply curious and adventurous person, so this trip shouldn't have surprised me. And it didn't; it *scared* me. All I could think was, *What if something bad happens to my daddy?* Meanwhile, he was thinking, *What if I stop letting myself live?*

One day, we look up and realize that our parents aren't just our parents. They are full, complicated human beings who have dreams, hopes, desires, fears, and equivocations. And they've always been those full human beings, struggling and wrestling to figure out who they are while they continually become it. All in front of us.

This reality brings such intense feelings. Most days we're thankful, other times disheartened or even disappointed in what we're learning about them. They never had it all together; hopefully they just did their best for us.

There are two distinct moments in life when most of us realize our parents are human. One, when we reach the age we can see their mistakes more clearly. You know—when you start to understand that it was their selfishness that messed up their marriage, or it's their social views that make you hesitant to bring anyone home.

Yeah . . . those times hurt.

The second one is when we see their bodies breaking down. They can no longer run as fast, jump as high, or protect us like they once could. We knew this time would come, that they wouldn't be able to put us on their shoulders anymore. Even still, knowing it would happen didn't make this reality any easier. The world as we know it morphs as this new, and unsettling world sets in. The gradual things begin to add up; it takes them a lot longer to get to the door, we see them trying to hide how poorly they're walking, or they're suddenly forgetting birthdays they've always been the first to remember. Watching it all unfold is a reckoning that unleashes a unique type of overwhelm, anxiety, and anticipatory grief.

It's so heavy, sometimes I think I can feel it in my bones. Can you?

We'd loved to think of our parents as impenetrable, safe, and all-knowing, when all along, they've only been human. Just like us.

Today, when they've hurt us, or just gotten scarily older, we can remember this. They were bound to fail us because they are just like us: messy, sometimes confused and unsure, just trying to figure out what the hell they should make for dinner. They don't know it all. They never did. We're *both* the people who know better but sometimes just don't do better, because we don't want to. (Maybe *that's* why they don't want to take their medication!) They are tired. They are concerned that the world they invested in building is failing us all. We want them to have all the answers, but they don't. Sometimes they are afraid. And of course they are, because as far as we know, we're all just doing life for the very first time.

On the days when it feels really hard to forgive them for their mistakes, we can remember that, in their humanity, our parents could only give us what they had. And yeah, what they gave may not have always filled our empty cups, yet somehow, by grace, we still made it.

It may be heartbreaking, but we need this truth so that our gentle hands can erect the boundaries that will protect our soft hearts. The distance between being a human and being a parent is filled with a lot of learning, a lot of mistakes, and a lot of imperfect teaching from the world. That gap doesn't close with our parents' perfection, but with managed expectations and careful understanding. Their intent didn't always match their impact, so we have to look to grace and accountability to guide us forward.

When we lose our confidence, looking at their aging bodies or cringeworthy social media posts, we reach for gratitude and whisper to ourselves, *This is hard as hell, but I'm still here, and they are, too. I will love them the best I can, even with distance, while loving myself in the process.*

You breathe. You retreat. You return.

Daily Invitations

Invitation to affirm

I feel this deeply because I care about them.
I can love the version they were and need space from the person they are now.
My feelings are messages, not my forever.
I am responsible for my choices, not theirs.
I do not have to carry this load alone.
Write your own: ______________________________

Invitation to reflect

What does it mean to not betray yourself as you care for them?
When it comes to your parents, what would give you more relief? (Space, boundaries, certainty, clarity, etc. Be as specific as possible.)
What would it look like to give your parents space to grow?
What would it mean to forgive your parents? Forgive yourself?

Invitation to commit

From today's soft landing:

The lesson I will take is ______________________.
The commitment I will make is ___________________.

SOFT LANDING #9

For the day your heart is broken

Blessed is the heart that breaks,
for it is a heart that has known love

I wonder, if you could do it again, would you still let them inside? Would you tell them your hidden truths? Would you let yourself be known by their love? Love, life's most potent gift, and you dared to open it. It rewarded you with new interpretations of simple pleasures. Suddenly, their hand under yours felt like a safety net. A shared meal was an escape from reality. In love, traffic was the blessing that gave you more time to daydream, and in love, distance was the friend that made your heart grow fonder.

Now, heartbroken, you wonder if it was worth it.

This is what happens when you dare to love.

The aftermath has been excruciating, the grief a weighted blanket. The happy laughs of strangers are like torrential rain distorting your vision, making it impossible for you to know where you're going. Some days, you feel so lost in this pain that you can't remember yourself without it. And to think you could have played it safe and ignored life's urging. But you were brave, and so now, here you are. You chose to *love*, and life rewarded you in a crushingly honest way.

You know loss because you know love.

You know fear because you know love.

You know yourself because you know love.

It's hard to appreciate it now, but this heartbreak gave you more evidence that you're living an abundant, complicated, and honest life. It's all happening to you, with every restless toss in bed and with every tear you shed. This pain is a witness to the power of your love and the intensity of your commitment. You got the gift of love, but wow, does this still hurt like hell. It hurts so, so badly. Like, make your lungs feel cloudy, cry in public, and don't care badly. You wonder how long you'll feel this way. Will it be weeks, months . . . a year? No one really knows. But if they did, they probably wouldn't tell you anyway. Don't worry; they didn't tell me either. You see, our unique healing journey is the best balm for our broken hearts. It's our road to walk.

Psalm 30 says there will be joy in your mourning. That means you may not be there yet, but one day soon you'll feel the persistence of your resilience and appreciate the integrity of your heart's wisdom. You will remember joy and discover a new purpose for this pain. You don't have to find it today, but you're on your way, and you're not alone. You are temporarily broken but, deep down, still determined. You sense it, like the seed that needs deep, dark soil before taking new root; you are rooting, all the while becoming something new because of the space in your broken heart. When you're ready, you will love again, and it will be amazing.

You didn't waste your time in love because you found yourself within it. And because love is the whole point of our time, you will never waste your time being in it. *Blessed is the heart that breaks, for it is a heart that has known love.*

Daily Invitations

Invitation to affirm

I will love again because I still love now.
My love is not done.
My life's love story has many chapters.
I can be broken in this moment and still hopeful for my future.
Blessed is my broken heart, for it is a heart that has known love.
Someone else knows how I feel.
Write your own: ____________________

Invitation to reflect

What does good self-care look like in this healing season?
How will you love yourself now?
What do you need?
How will you give yourself what you need?
Who needs to support you? How will you invite them in?

Invitation to commit

From today's soft landing:

The lesson I will take is ____________________________.

The commitment I will make is ________________________.

SOFT LANDING #10

For the day it feels like you're grieving alone

We have walked them home,
but somehow our journey continues

The day you found out, it felt like the world stopped. The calls were numerous, and the care felt palpable. There was more food than you had an appetite for, and the random check-ins felt consistent. But now, time has passed, and it seems the world has moved on. The immediate flurry of activity has waned, and the mundanity of everyday life feels like a cruel joke. Why is everyone acting like things are the same? For you, everything is different. The loneliness of the midnight hour has turned into twenty-five hours. Does anyone know the hell you're in? Does anyone still care?

But one day, somehow, in the stillness of it all, you will manage to hear the Comforter match your breath. "In and out," the Spirit says. "Breathe with me—in and out. Do you feel that? That's me.

I'm still here. I knew you would need me, and that's why I didn't leave you. I know you are in the depths of despair, and I promise I'll be here with you. Don't worry about doing more than you can right now. Only do what I offer you . . . one moment at a time. If that's a breath, take that. If that's a step, take that.

"I know this sucks. And I know it hurts like hell. But I promise you are not forgotten. You are my child, and I know exactly where you are. I have taken what you loved for now, but not forever. In time, the memories will bring more smiles than tears. They are with me, and so are you. You are both so loved."

YOU'RE GLAD TO know you're not alone because it feels like you have so far to go.

You have walked them home, and impossibly your journey continues. I know you may never move on, but in time, slowly, with grace, you will move forward. Even if it's inch by inch. What do you need to take the next step? Is it more grace? More space? More love? What do you need to ask for? Your grief is the love that needs a new home. What do you need in this home?

Take your time and ask for what you need. This isn't yours to carry alone.

There is no rush to return to a world that's forever changed.

Here is a prayer for your grieving heart:

Oh God, give me doses of joy I can still swallow.

I know things will never be the same, so give me the strength to find the good in what's left.

Help me notice and embrace the good that still exists.

Give me helpers for the journey and people who aren't afraid to sit with me while I'm in this hell. Join me in my cave of sadness, and with your light, remind me that I am never alone.

Daily Invitations

Invitation to affirm

I am not alone in this grief.
I do not have to walk this road alone.
I grieve because I love.
My grief reminds me I'm still here.
Write your own: ______________________________

Invitation to reflect

What do you need today?
What is one step you will take to meet this need?
What support do you need from your community?

Invitation to commit

From today's soft landing:

The lesson I will take is ______________________.
The commitment I will make is __________________.

When We Need to Remember We Are Worthy

Sit with me.

Every day, the world is telling us that we're not quite good enough. We need more of this, or we should have already done that. All around us, there are sinkholes of shame that threaten to bring us down. We're pretty good at avoiding those traps, but some days we need to be reminded that we are good. That we are capable. That we are worthy.

In this series of soft landings, we're reminded of our worthiness. Together, let's tap into reservoirs of resilience and streams of encouragement.

SOFT LANDING #11

For the day it's hard to start something new

To live is to keep beginning

Award-winning composer Hans Zimmer once said that at the beginning of every project, he still stares with terror at a blank page, afraid people will finally find out he has no idea what he's doing. Yes, this is the same Hans Zimmer who scored films like *Gladiator*, *The Lion King*, and *The Dark Knight*. And even after all that, he's still afraid, like us, to begin again.

Maybe you're starting a new career path, dating again after a divorce, going back to school, or beginning a new health routine. You know you've been in this place before—the "beginning" of something new—but today, you're feeling so anxious it's hard to remember what you did last time.

It's easy to forget because this time it feels like there is much more on the line—so much at stake. But that was then, and this is now. You worked hard to get here, and you don't want to lose it.

And even though you earned this spot, the newness of it all feels unsettling and nerve-racking. You're tempted to shrink back into your shell. It feels like you have more to prove and much less grace to hold.

But when you get still, you can hear your spirit get curious: *This may be a new experience, but is it really that different?*

Your spirit is onto something, because it's not that different. The context may have changed, but some things are still true:

You worked for this.

You earned these nerves.

You're prepared for this moment because of every nervous moment before it.

You're ready for this. You may not know the exact outcome, but you don't need to, because *you know who you are.* You're smart, capable, intrepid, creative, discerning, generous, innovative, disciplined, focused, and determined. And today, most importantly, you're a learner worthy of grace.

You can begin again, just like you always have.

You're ready to begin again when you remember that progress is better than perfection. You don't have to be right on day one, just committed to getting it right over time.

You can keep living.

It's easy to feel like a fraud when you're trying to be someone you're not. But today isn't that. Right now, you're simply beginning again. Any disruptive impostor energy is connected to the lies you've been told about success. Your job is to make sure you don't believe them. These lies sound like:

Once you've reached the top, you can't try something new.

You can't make mistakes.

You should know all "this" by now.

You will fail beyond another chance.

Lies like these want to shrink and confine you. But the truth will always liberate you. The truth is:

No matter how many mistakes you've made, you deserve grace to make another one.

No matter how much success you've had, you have permission to try something new.

No matter how old you are, you can never outgrow the need to start over.

With every new job, relationship, hairstyle, or venture you've shown that you can trust yourself to begin again. Today is no different.

Now take a deep breath, settle into the truth and keep living. It's time to begin again.

Daily Invitations

An invitation to affirm

I give myself permission to be a beginner.

I will take the opportunity to try something new.

I will take the opportunity to "see what happens."

I will apply my trusted skills to a new opportunity.

Write your own: ________________________________

An invitation to reflect

Where do you need to give yourself grace?

What does beginning again look like?

What will help you begin again well?

Where do you need support?

An invitation to commit

From today's soft landing:

The lesson I will take is ______________________________.

The commitment I will make is _______________________.

SOFT LANDING #12

For the day your mistake holds you hostage

Mistakes don't ruin credibility; they inform it

You look at the email that's been sitting in your draft folder, the email you thought you sent a week ago. You shake your head in disappointment, realizing this email is the reason the project is over budget and delayed two weeks. You've made a mistake. But I promise it's not just you. Undoubtedly, at the same time, someone else forgot the gift bags for their son's party, and another person didn't finish the Instacart order they thought was being delivered.

Everywhere, every day, all of us are making some type of mistake. They may vary in size, and their consequences may be different, but the feelings they evoke can be the same: shame, disappointment, embarrassment, even confusion. In a parallel universe, we wouldn't have made the mistake. We would have gone left instead of right; we would have checked our payment before closing the app. But as far as we know, we're only living in this universe. And today, in this universe, making this mistake feels pretty frustrating.

It feels like you need to prove you're worthy, like you need to shed the shame before you decide of how you'll move forward. You're stuck at the site of the mistake, replaying in your mind the good things that would've happened had you just gotten it right the first time.

You only know a world where the mistake happened, and now you have to figure out your way forward.

Enter grace.

There's no heavenly badge for people who never needed grace, but there's a heaven on earth for those of us who knew we needed it all along. Now, when your shame wants to hold you hostage, you have to break out of its cell and let yourself be brought into a hug of grace and worthiness. You have to speak to the younger versions of yourself tucked inside you. They are still wondering, *Is it okay to make mistakes? And if you make them, how do you recover?*

So what are you going to tell them? You can tell them that you're still a candidate for redemption. You can tell them, sure, you forgot the gift bags, but you can still figure out plans B and C. You can tell them that sometimes the things we don't plan for end up being the best things to happen.

If you let yourself see mistakes as a growth point, an opportunity to learn, you can make your mistakes matter. You can give your mistakes a purpose. In life, we often see that mistakes don't ruin credibility; they inform it. We believe in people who are real enough to make mistakes and bold enough to tell us what they learned. Their honesty creates genuine connection.

When you see your mistakes as natural and even to be expected, you can recover faster. And that's the key: You have to recover.

I know today feels like it'd be better spent if you just let the mistake swallow you whole. But what if you did like Dr. Thema Bryant says, and you take "wisdom from the wound"? In this way, you might even begin to collect your mistakes like seashells, things to help you remember your adventures and where you've been. Just like the scars that are on your body. Remember that scar that's on your right arm, the one you got when you were moving too fast? It reminds you to move slowly. If you think about your mistakes as your teachers, I wonder, which one has been your favorite?

You have so much to tell the younger versions of yourself. You can start by telling them that self-compassion and loving accountability are the first steps in moving forward. You can tell them that mistakes might be events, but they are never your identity, and they will never be.

Hopefully you're starting to feel better, and slowly but surely, all of this is starting to sink in. When you're ready, you can rub a hand over your heart and say: *I am still the young soul learning what it means to be the imperfectly perfect me.*

Daily Invitations

An invitation to affirm

I'm already recovering from my mistake.

Making a mistake doesn't make me a mistake.

I release my shame so I can reclaim my worthiness.

Write your own: ________________________________

An invitation to reflect

What is still possible for me now?

What does grace look like for me?

How have I honored accountability?

What is my work to do?

What is a reasonable, accessible next step?

An invitation to commit

From today's soft landing:

The lesson I will take is ________________________.

The commitment I will make is ____________________.

SOFT LANDING #13

For the day you're afraid to ask for what you deserve

You're worthy of the best

"It sure would be nice to have some ice cream, Mama."

I looked down to see my daughter, a newly five-year-old Jorgie, looking up at me with more suspicion than hope. I turned to the microwave to check the time. It was 3:15 p.m. I did a quick cost-benefit analysis and considered the facts of the day—it's a no-nap Saturday, and our family movie night would start in a few hours. I found myself leaning toward a yes but suddenly realized she didn't *actually* ask me for anything. She was hedging her bets, preparing for a no. She thought that if she whispered her request, my potential denial might not sound so loud.

"You're right, it would be nice," I replied matter-of-factly. Jorgie looked at me curiously.

"Well?"

"Well, what, honey? You didn't ask me for anything. If you

want some ice cream, you can ask for it with confidence. You don't need to whisper. Say it like you mean it, like you deserve it. It may not change my answer, but it'll let me know you're serious about it."

She growled in frustration and quickly walked away to re-strategize her approach. Giving her the ice cream would have been easier, but I knew the lesson would have been lost: *Believe you are worthy of the best thing.*

The world is coming for Jorgie, just like it's come for us. The same world that's deflated our spirits by denying our rightful promotions and systematically gaslighting our success. The world that's urged us to dim and contort, so often that at times we've lost our shine and shape. But even worse, we've almost lost the belief that we are worthy.

This is the world that's manipulated you into thinking that if you ask for half, you'll be more likely to get a yes. And if you make yourself small, maybe you won't disturb too many people. I know you've been doing cultural strategy as a means of self-preservation, and it's started to diminish your sense of worth. But it's not your fault—you've just been trying to survive. But I bet you're tired of just surviving. Especially because you know you were born to thrive. And that thriving starts with remembering that you deserve the very best.

Let's admit to each other it's not easy recovering from the last no that almost broke our heart. How many times do they expect us to rebound? How many times do *we* expect it? We've seen our mothers deny themselves a soft landing, and we come from generations who were told they should "just be happy to be here."

To survive the traumas of this world, you've smoothed your

rough edges—not for your own soft landings but to create them for others. But how long do they expect you to deny the dignity and love that is your birthright? You need your things. You need the funding, promotion, support. You need an empathetic witness to your pain. It's infuriating, really, knowing, not deep down but right here on the surface, that you deserve the *very best*. Knowing you have what it takes. Knowing you've been worthy since birth.

Hmmmmm, I feel it. Something is shifting, isn't it?

You're starting to believe again. Scary for them, but I think you just remembered how dope you are. How undeniable you can be. How inevitable you are. They said your arms weren't meant to reach space, but you've already started to grab your stars. You just remembered your self-advocacy is an act of self-love that'll take you beyond this world.

They're so comfortable when you don't ask for what's yours. But you have to stop keeping their peace when your soft landing depends on your fight. Maybe today, your soft landing is in letting your anger resonate into confident action. Asking for what you deserve, not because you know they'll finally say yes, but because you'll never stop believing that they should. And if you get tired, it's okay. You can just take a breath. Take it with me. Take it with your friends. We're in this together.

Breathe in confidence and exhale delusion.

Breathe in worthiness and exhale insecurity.

And breathe in gratitude and exhale lack.

Repeat this as often as you want.

And with every breath, think to yourself, *I deserve the very best thing.*

Daily Invitations

An invitation to affirm

I am worthy of good things.
I can and will ask for what I deserve.
I deserve goodness in my life.
My good life doesn't have to ruin theirs.
Write your own: ______________________________

An invitation to reflect

What do you need to ask for?
How can you affirm your worthiness today?
What do you believe about yourself?
What are your secret superpowers?

An invitation to commit

From today's soft landing:

The lesson I will take is ________________________.
The commitment I will make is ____________________.

SOFT LANDING #14

For the day you're overthinking it

You can't edit what's not created

After years of living in quaint New York City apartments, having turned corners into home offices and, even more recently, having turned my office into Jorgie's nursery, you can imagine how excited I was to have a permanent home office. When we moved into our new house, I went to HomeGoods and bought art pieces for my wall. I was determined to hang them.

I remember unpacking each picture with a smile, leaning them against the wall. As I held one up to the space that would eventually be its home, I squealed to no one, "This is going to be so dope!!!" I placed that picture next to the others, promising to hang them once I had the clear vision, tools, and energy to do so. Months went by and the pictures sat by the couch, unhung. In the beginning I would look at them and smile, but as time moved on, I began to roll my eyes in frustration.

One Tuesday, I sat in my cozy corner, wrapping up a session

with my longtime therapist, when I caught a glimpse of the pictures. I mentioned that I was frustrated that they hadn't been hung.

"Why haven't they been hung?" she asked plainly.

"Because I don't know how they should be hung. . . . and if I mess it up, I'll have to start over or fix it." My tone said all but "Duh."

"What's wrong with that?" she asked with a slow smile.

I leaned back into a pillow, slightly embarrassed at my tone and how obvious the answer now seemed. The answer was that nothing was wrong with starting over, nothing was wrong with wasting time on this, and nothing was wrong with a messy first attempt. Ironically, I'd already wasted time being too scared of wasting time or getting it wrong. Now sure, I could've asked George to hang them, or even hired someone, both of which I had done in the past, but this wasn't about that. *This was about how I let the idea of getting it wrong stop me from even trying to get it right.*

Is that where you are right now?

Days like today, you want things to be so good that you judge a final product that hasn't even been made. You begin to overthink your steps. You might feel overly judgmental, insecure, and nervous about your choices. You think their idea is better than yours so why should you even try. The desire to get it right stops you from taking the first step, and the fear of wasting time stops you from enjoying the journey. This can happen to us all, and when it does, it's clear that somewhere along the way, we have forgotten:

You can't fix what doesn't exist.

You can't edit what hasn't been created.

And you can't expand what isn't built.

When I started writing, my dad would often tell me, "Perfection is the enemy of finished." He's right. Days like today, when you're overthinking your steps, trying to make sure each one is right, you have to remember that you just need to take a step. It doesn't have to be the right step; it just has to *be a step*. There's no final draft without the first draft. And today, you need permission to make that ugly first draft.

Herein lies the power of the ugly first draft: Because of it, you can begin to make sense of your vision. You can see what works and what doesn't. You can experiment and try new things! And with every "mistake" you make along the way? Every scratch on the wall, every spelling error? You only become more powerful. Each misstep is a lesson and a teacher. The imperfection doesn't make you untrustworthy but more informed. It's in your attempts that your resilience erupts and your self-trust strengthens.

It's in your pivot, not your perfection, that you show yourself what you're learning.

Our soft landing is in how we give ourselves the space and grace to find the beauty in the journey and the "right" over time. It's not in the incessant edits or overwhelming critiques; it's in our discovery along the way. Our soft landing is in how we move away from overthinking ourselves into decision fatigue, and into meditating ourselves into courageous vulnerability.

When you're overthinking it, you're likely not living it. And today, my friend, it's time you start living again.

Daily Invitations

An invitation to affirm

I trust me, with me.
What I don't get right now, I will learn from later.
I am proud of my progress.
Write your own: ______________________________

An invitation to reflect

What is one thing you're wondering if you should create, submit, turn in, or publish?
What is a meaningful next step you can take?
What does progress look like?

An invitation to commit

From today's soft landing:

The lesson I will take is ______________________.
The commitment I will make is __________________.

SOFT LANDING #15

For the day you doubt your ability

Don't waste your expert years acting like a beginner

I was a decade into my career as a keynote speaker when I found myself spiraling with insecurity and doubt. I was two days out from a major speaking engagement, but I hadn't received the preparation documents from the client. I was frustrated and nervous, and lamented to my therapist that given this timeline, I wouldn't have sufficient time to prepare and meet my dad, who was in town for dinner.

Context: For years, I've hung my hat on being extra prepared, memorizing my keynotes so I can stand confidently with no notes or screens, and practicing for hours in front of mirrors so I can cover the stage with ease. I had done some prep for this engagement, but I still felt that without my normal routine, I wasn't going to be that good.

"Okay," my therapist said. "What are they interviewing you about?"

"Purpose, leadership, and transitions," I replied.

"I suppose you know a thing or ten about that," she smirked. I rolled my eyes and laughed.

"Definitely."

"So, tell me a few things you'd want to share with this audience. Tell me about your key points and research," she directed.

I jumped in, telling her about a few frameworks and research studies I was eager to share. After a few minutes, she lovingly interrupted me.

"You did that fairly easily, almost as if you'd done it hundreds of times before. What I heard from you was a clear point of view on this topic. And no, you don't know everything, but hell, who does? You have informative and incisive thoughts that you *and* your client believe would be valuable for this audience. What I'm sensing is that you're worried that if you don't follow your normal routine, you may not have success. You're trusting your routine more than yourself. But Jovian, *don't waste your expert years acting like you're a beginner.* When you were a beginner, you needed all that prep, but now that you've done it a thousand times, you might need something different."

Whoa. She was right. I hung up feeling more confident.

At some point in our lives, we move from beginner to expert. Our years of experience inform our decision-making and leadership, both in our homes and in our careers. When we're hired to do something, we aren't just giving the four hours we'll spend on a project—we're providing thousands of hours of past study, research, practice, failure, and growth that's prepared us for the moment.

The transition from beginner to expert happens in stages. Sometimes we understand it through titles or promotions, but other times it's more subtle, like when we realize something that used to take us days to complete now only takes us a few hours. When this transition comes, we have to recognize it. Even more, we have to honor it.

Of course, it's not always easy. Some days you doubt your ability because your experience is different from others. Sometimes you doubt it because the conditions around you have changed. (I'm thinking about the time they hired you and then changed your job description!) On these days, you can feel too nervous to share your ideas or begin to overthink your contributions. You might find yourself second-guessing your every move because of environments that reinforce negative feedback, gaslighting, and unhealthy competition. And when you do, the soft landing is to *be skeptical of the environment while being gentle with yourself.* You can take your time to decide how long you want to "squeeze that lemon" before you take your glass of lemonade elsewhere. You don't need to stay in a place or relationship you've outgrown.

Today, as an expert, you're reminded that in the face of loud doubt, you have to turn up your truths. You have to let yourself evolve into who you need to be. And maybe you're being called not just to reinvent the wheel but to introduce new shapes.

Daily Invitations

An invitation to affirm

I can do things differently.
I can be an expert without being omniscient.
I don't need to prove myself in every situation.
My abilities are going to change.
I am capable of being effective, making mistakes, and still adding value.
Write your own: ________________________________

An invitation to reflect

How and where have you experienced doubt in your abilities?
What were the conditions?
What is the source of your doubt?
What is the source of your truth?
In the area where you have doubt, what is your qualitative and quantitative impact? What are your areas of expertise? What is your future desired impact?

An invitation to commit

From today's soft landing:

The lesson I will take is ________________________.
The commitment I will make is ____________________.

When We Need Help Honoring the Seasons of Our Lives

Sit with me.

Life is mercurial. The moment we're finally comfortable with one thing, it can very easily change. Honoring each season is necessary, but it is not always easy. Sometimes we need help identifying the season we're in, and we need help finding comfort within it. Join me as we find our way to a soft landing through life's changing seasons.

SOFT LANDING #16

For the day you miss your old life

That time may be gone, but you're still here

Around my daughter Jorgie's third birthday, I felt a wave of unmistakable grief. I categorically, undeniably, missed my old life. Yes, I was grateful for the new life that I had—the life that I had *prayed* for. And yet, I still missed aspects of my old life. I missed the independence and freedom that marked the years I'd spent living in New York City. I missed the casual run-ins with friends and the all-day bottomless mimosa brunches. The "get up and go because I wanted to" years. The years I didn't have to coordinate with the calendar before getting a manicure, and didn't have to secure a sitter before going out to dinner. I missed the time in my life when the only person I had to take care of was me. To complicate matters, I didn't just miss this stuff—I felt shitty about missing it in the first place. I'd heard from other parents that this feeling would come, but it didn't make it any less difficult to process.

As we all evolve into new dimensions of ourselves it can be hard—admitting we still miss something we were ready to leave behind. It can feel like an ugly admission of selfishness or ingratitude. And on top of that, how dare we miss things that we willingly gave up only to then get what so many people want? Are we grateful or delusional?

Maybe you're like I was for a long time, denying your feelings. I did this because, like many women, I was socialized to be nice before being honest. But to find our peace, we need to tell the truth. *There's no soft landing in our lies.*

What if missing parts of your old life doesn't make you a bad person, an ungrateful partner, or a selfish leader? What if it just makes you human? You're allowed to miss things, especially the things you worked so hard to build. You miss them because they were *that* good. And you miss them because they once meant *that much*. Is it possible to miss something without returning to it? Definitely. You can be grateful for what you have and still miss aspects of what was.

There's a soft landing when we let our feelings inform us instead of judge us. Sometimes the things we miss give us insight into the things we still need. I still need my independence and moments of feeling carefree. It took some effort, certainly more than it used to, but with intention I began to experience familiar independence and freedom again.

Friend, what do you miss? What do you still need? I'll sit here while you tell yourself the truth.

I know it's hard to transition with ease. So many big changes are often colored by a tidal wave of mixed emotions, sometimes regret, resentment, or grief. Sometimes missing the past feels less sudden and more like a slow erosion of old comforts. But thankfully, new seasons can also bring renewed joy, courage, and contentment. Today, when you miss what was, the old life that gave you so much, you're allowed to feel the swirl of confusing and conflicting emotions. They are real and they are yours.

It's okay to be grateful and sad. To be hopeful and unsure. The "both and" is your truth, and it's the nuance that makes up your very real, very honest, and very beautiful life.

Daily Invitations

An invitation to affirm

My feelings are indicators, not indictments.
I have the capacity to feel many things at once.
The things I miss remind me that I have loved.
I will continue to love.

An invitation to reflect

What do you feel?
How are your feelings informing your new needs?
What is the story you're telling yourself? (Identify any limiting beliefs.)
What do you appreciate about the past season(s)?
What do you appreciate about your current life? (Get as specific and relevant as possible.)

An invitation to commit

From today's soft landing:

The lesson I will take is ______________________.
The commitment I will make is ___________________.

SOFT LANDING #17

For the day your body betrays you

Give your body grace

I was thirteen when my body first betrayed me. While the rest of the eighth grade was huddled in the cafeteria rehearsing lines for our class play, I was locked in the last stall of the girls' bathroom, desperately fending off incoming pit stains—stuffing paper towels in the armpits of my costume. But it was too late. I knew I would be made fun of. Maybe not to my face, but the whispers and notes would be passed. My suspicions were correct, and years later, I found a yearbook where my "friends" had written a joke about me. It hurt like salt in a wound.

It sucks when you feel betrayed by people you love, but there's a unique kind of sting when your own body has let you down. The doctor gives you a life-defining diagnosis. You're running and out of nowhere your left hip gives out. Or you're wearing all white and suddenly your period comes early. It can all feel like betrayal. The depth of the betrayal just depends on how much trust has been broken and how much is at stake. Did a fart slip out during a first date? Did you get the flu the day before your wedding? Did the doctor confirm that the cancer had returned?

Sometimes the disappointment is too much to bear.

When your body doesn't do what it *used* to do, what you *want* it to do, or what you *thought* it would do, it's hard not to feel betrayed. It's like a sacred trust has been violated. Suddenly, you must confess to everyone that the trust has been broken. A public admission you weren't ready to share.

Our relationship with our bodies is fraught. When our ability, physical or cognitive, doesn't align with our desires, we can feel caged—trapped behind the bars of our limitations. Whether it's temporary or chronic, the limitation of a new diagnosis forces us to rethink even the most routine habits. Days like today, when you're in the midst of betrayal, you want to replay what you used to take for granted. The day sleep *actually* felt peaceful. The day you didn't need assistance to do your hair. Or the day you didn't have to take pills just to think. It's all so jarring, disorienting, and frustrating. We can be sure that over time our bodies will change and often through these changes, it feels like it is failing us. We suddenly can't eat spicy foods, we can't play basketball without spraining an ankle, or spin around without getting dizzy.

Maybe you knew today was coming, signs of inevitability around you like breadcrumbs. But maybe today feels like a complete surprise. You've tried to nurture your body, giving it good foods, vitamins, and routines. And in many ways, your body has faithfully adjusted through every other change, but somehow this change feels different. You body, your forever home has let down.

So what do you do when it betrays you? When your home is crumbling, or at the very least in need of repair. You start with the truth: *Your body has changed, and now, so will you.* It's okay to grieve your body of before. You grieve because you love, and because you appreciate what was. To move past betrayal, you have to decide if the relationship is worth repairing. Will you forgive your body? Will you thank your body for what it's done? Will you look ahead at what can be, rather than idolizing what was?

Let yourself dream a new dream. There's a softer place to land when you release the shame of betrayal and you allow yourself to honor the present. The path to a soft landing requires bravery, agape love, and vulnerability.

Bravery: Lean into bravery so you can find a courageous faith that says, *I can love this body as it is and as it will be.*

Agape Love: Lean into agape love so you can treat your body compassionately, with new routines, habits, and fresh forgiveness.

Vulnerability: Lean into vulnerability so you can ask for help to love and evolve gracefully through the uncertainty, emotional exposure, and risk of a changing body.

It takes a brave person to love their body through its changes. It takes a compassionate person to love their body's imperfections. And it takes a courageously vulnerable person to seek help along the way. The good news? You are already all of those things.

Daily Invitations

An invitation to affirm

My body is still my friend.

I can rebuild trust with my body.

My body has brought me this far, and I am grateful.

Write your own: ________________________________

An invitation to reflect

Identify one nice thing you want to do for your body today.

What support do you need?

What could help you trust your body again?

An invitation to commit

From today's soft landing:

The lesson I will take is ____________________________.

The commitment I will make is ______________________.

SOFT LANDING #18

For the day it feels like you've run out of time

Release your grip on imaginary timelines

Some years ago, before Jorgie was born, I found myself in the San Francisco airport, preparing to head home after a successful work trip. I sat content, absolutely demolishing a bowl of chips and salsa, when I noticed a beautiful family walk by. That was all it took to remind me that my life was behind schedule.

I immediately called my mom; she often knows what to say. I caught her up on my work, the reason I was even in San Francisco, and I could feel her smile through the phone. But in a way that only a mother's intuition can, she paused just long enough for my heart to catch up to my words. Seemingly out of left field, I blurted out, "Mama, I'm worried that I missed my chance. What if George and I can't get pregnant? What if I've run out of time?!" Long pause. "Mama?"

"I'm here, sweet pea. What do you mean, run out of time?"

"I mean, I'm in my mid-thirties, and I don't have a kid. I'm so late into my childbearing window. I'm just hitting my stride in my career, and I don't know when or how I can do both. I want to be pregnant! But what if when I try, it doesn't happen for me? I think I'm already too late!" Tears welled in my eyes.

My mom took her time responding and slowly said, "Oh, Jovian, I hear you, honey. I understand you're worried and we will pray in a minute. But I first want to say, it sounds like you have a tight grip on your timeline for things. You're holding on to your ideas of *when* things should happen, and *how* they should happen. In my experience, it's better to release your grip on these things and hold hands with God instead."

I'd apparently been holding my breath, because when she finished, I exhaled for way longer than I expected.

"Wheeeeewww, that's a good one, Mama."

I bet today you've been holding your breath, too. So worried that you've missed the boat. Concerned that you're too old, or too far behind to catch up to your dream. Sometimes this anxiety makes your worries feel more real than the things you can touch. You secretly pledged allegiance to a deadline. But you've held too tight, and now your fingers are numb and you can't feel the power of other dreams coming true.

Here's what you have to remember: *Life doesn't happen on society's timeline, not even our own.* Life unfolds at the Universe's pace, one divinely ordered and prepared. And even still, it's big and wild enough to let us choose our own adventures. Life isn't a video game to play, and there are no levels we need to hit. But when we treat it like this, we play ourselves in the process.

We can be thoughtful and strategic without putting our dreams on a clock. Things may not always come at the time we want them, but undoubtedly, they always come on time. When we release our grip on "what should be," we can take hold of what actually is. But if we don't, we run a great risk.

When we don't release our grip on the world's definition of success, we won't be satisfied with the purpose in every season.

When we don't release our grip, we won't appreciate the things we've worked hard to accomplish.

When we don't release our grip, we put an asterick before meaningful moments, docking them because they were "late."

Close your eyes and tune out the noise. You are right where you need to be. You are on time for your wonderful life.

Daily Invitations

An invitation to affirm

I am on time for the life I am creating.
I am cocreating what's next.
My life is unfolding as it should.
Write your own: ______________________________

An invitation to reflect

Who gave you the timeline you're holding on to?
How is your current timeline serving you?
Name one deadline you need to release.
With free hands, what will you pick up instead?

An invitation to commit

From today's soft landing:

The lesson I will take is ______________________________.

The commitment I will make is ________________________.

SOFT LANDING #19

For the day your life needs pruning

Not every flower belongs in your garden

When's the last time you gave yourself a cosmic reset? The kind of blow-in-the-cartridge type of reboot that removes life's cobwebs. It takes pruning shears to our lives, removing overrun plants that are stopping us from blooming where we're planted. This type of reset is self-care in nature, as it helps us rethink our priorities, relationships, and how we're using our time.

Every so often, we get a reminder that it's time to reset. Sometimes the reminder is a gentle prodding; other times it sounds like a roar. Mine came as a roar, or more accurately said, my own wailing.

One Mother's Day, George got me a massage from a world-class masseuse. I was ready to relax. Before getting started, the masseuse asked, "Are there any tension areas I should know about?"

I responded casually, "Yeah, my hips and my back, but it's not too bad." I closed my eyes, determined to ease into relaxation.

Two minutes into the massage, she slowed down and said, "Hey love, you have an incredible amount of tension in your shoulders. A lot of stress is bottled here. Do you know what's causing so much stress?"

Knowing I was being watched, I forced myself (well, tried) to relax my shoulders as I rattled off my laundry list of mental and physical responsibilities. I was embarrassed to be so stressed. I knew better. But more than feeling embarrassed, I was sad. Before I knew it, tears were flowing, and a small puddle was forming on the floor. I kept thinking, *How did I get here?* My massage was an ironic, not-so-gentle alarm that whatever I'd been doing to take care of myself in that season wasn't working.

It's hard to admit when your life's garden has become overrun. Especially when your garden is full of things you love. But life is seasonal, and some flowers can't survive winter.

You're here today because you sense your life needs pruning, or perhaps thinning. It needs you to remove the stuff that looks good but is starting to weigh you down.

One day I was on FaceTime with my mom, proudly showing her my plants. She said, "You need to cut the weeds off your basil, honey."

"What weeds?" I said, confused.

"You see those white flowers? They aren't meant to be there. If you let them, they will overrun the herb."

I hesitated because the flowers looked so pretty. Could they really be that bad? But the pretty flowers were still weeds. *And even pretty weeds can damage healthy plants.* If I didn't prune the bush, the basil leaves would have no space to thrive.

The basil plant is us. The pretty flowers are the things holding us back, the things we've carried into new seasons that should've been left behind. The friendship that's run its course, the committee we need to leave, or the routine we need to change. It's also the expectations that need to be reset, the responsibilities we should delegate, and the people we need to stop trying to please.

The seasonality of life is urging you to reevaluate and reconcile what you're still holding on to. In this season, do the things that once felt light suddenly feel too heavy? Has the pressure intensified? Conditions change in new seasons, and so might the priorities in your life. What if, in this season, you are:

Called to do less with more?

Asked to give the little you have to yourself?

Meant to end one relationship so you can make space for another?

In some seasons, even the things you've always done well are no longer yours to do. The trick is not to compare seasons or become distracted by what you used to do. That could lead to toxic comparison or burnout.

Today, when your life needs pruning, what will you put down so you can pick up some peace? What are you willing to prune? As you pick up your shears, don't be afraid to start with the pretty weeds.

Daily Invitations

An invitation to affirm

I can reset my priorities.
I will respect my needs.
I will prune as an act of self-love.
Write your own: ______________________________

An invitation to reflect

In this season, what are my priorities?
How do I know what is a priority?
How do my current priorities support me in being the person I was created to be?
What do I need to prune in this season?
What needs more space to grow?

An invitation to commit

From today's soft landing:

The lesson I will take is ________________________.
The commitment I will make is ____________________.

SOFT LANDING #20

For the day comparison has stolen your joy

Never let their green grass stop you from watering your own

It's 9 p.m. and you're exhausted from a long day. As long as it was, your day was filled with things you love. You successfully wrapped a major project at work. You caught up with friends at happy hour and got to watch the first half of the game. You talked to both your parents and they sounded well, thank God. You're pleased with your meal choices for the day, and you even remembered to take your vitamins. "Life is good," you say aloud. A feeling of contentment washes over you as you plop on the couch and open your phone. Your thumb instinctively opens Instagram for a quick scroll: A friend's promotion . . . a wedding recap . . . Dani got a new house . . . *Wait, how did they get tickets to that concert—I thought it was sold out?* . . . A semi-inspirational quote . . . a baby putts a hole in one . . . the Lakers lost the game in

OT on free throws. The more you swipe, the more you start to feel unsettled—your feeling of contentment quickly fading. Your dog comes over with his leash, reminding you that you still have one more thing to do. You roll your eyes, huff, and pull yourself off the couch.

It was all good, a couple of swipes ago. You didn't do anything except open your phone and look "outside." But that quick look was all it took to pop a dormant insecurity like a pimple: *Maybe my good life isn't that good after all.*

Unfortunately, the times we need reassurance that we're on the right path—that we didn't veer too far off our cosmic course, that our life is still good—we tend to look outside of our *knowing*. We look at others' lives instead of our own. We scroll through timelines instead of our own memories, the memories that would remind us that just yesterday we picked kale from our garden and last month we took a trip of a lifetime. We swipe during our most vulnerable moments, putting our eyes to a broken telescope. But a broken telescope won't show us the truth of the skies. It distorts what we see and makes us question the size of our planet. *When will we stop going to broken places to fix our broken parts?*

Comparison is a parasite determined to suck the gratitude out of your life. Suddenly, nothing feels good enough. Not even the degree you paid thousands of dollars to earn, or the partner you went on thirty-four dates to find. Comparison changes your perspective, dissolving your appreciation into resentment and your joy into casual acknowledgment.

What's out there isn't always the full story, and their highlight reels can pull you further from contentment and closer to frustration. Here's the truth: *You can't get clarity from a cracked screen, and you can't get confirmation from a distorted reality.*

It's normal to look for reassurance. You just want to know, like we all do, that your life, as you've designed it, is good enough. You want to be assured that every sacrifice, tough choice, and commitment was worth it. You want to know that your life is good.

But wait, you *do* know it. You know your life is good. You, with your courageous self, have made bold choices, and they've all been worth it—even the times you fell on your face. Every choice, by grace, has been redeemed or confirmed. You don't need to compare your good life.

Try to remember this: A society that struggles to reconcile its obsession with materialism and consumption can't be trusted to love you well. It'll never know what's best for you in the way that you do. That's why you have to:

Trust what you know.

Love what you've made.

Be grateful for what you've been given.

You decided you didn't want kids, and you're waiting for the rest of the world to be okay with it. You knew a return to grad school made sense, even if they didn't think the loans were worth it. People say your talent is made for a bigger city, but you feel perfectly placed in your city, in the tight-knit community you've worked hard to create. You know bigger isn't always better, and more isn't always manageable. You feel good about the life you've rightsized to match your dreams and your well-being. *You are proud of your good life.*

When it's time for something different, you'll do it on your terms and in your own way. Until then, be grateful for what is.

You don't need me, your mama, or anyone else to confirm what you already know—you have a damn good life. And that good life of yours? It deserves your gratitude and attention.

Daily Invitations

An invitation to affirm

I've built a life I enjoy.
I'll continue to create my good life.
I won't let their green grass stop me from watering my own.
I am proud of myself.
Write your own: ______________________________

An invitation to reflect

How would you describe this season of life?
How can you protect your contentment?
What's one brave choice that led to the good life you have today?
What do you want to celebrate?
You are the main character of your life's journey. Name one amazing aspect of your journey: ____________________.

An invitation to commit

From today's soft landing:

The lesson I will take is ____________________.
The commitment I will make is ____________________.

When We Hunger to Appreciate Life's Goodness

Sit with me.

In hard times, appreciating life's goodness isn't easy, especially if we aren't trained to see it. In some seasons we can see the goodness all around us but still have a hard time believing it's happening to us. So, for the moments when life is generous but you still can't find the grace to enjoy them, settle into the next few chapters for some familiar good days that could still use a soft landing.

SOFT LANDING #21

For the day you fall in love

Your heart is ready, and so are you

Even though you've always had love, falling into this love feels different. Where love once felt like an escape from reality, this time, love is helping you realize who you were always meant to be. In your discipline to love, you are learning how to pick your battles and how to leave space for forgiveness. This love is a guide, protectively ushering you through life's ups and downs. This love isn't a hobby; it's a grounding.

You see, that's what love does. It walks you home to yourself. In love, you discover new gifts, like patience and creativity. And superpowers, like perspective and resilience. Love is the ultimate giver. Love is the ultimate companion.

In love, there's a new sense of urgency, too. Real love makes you want to live more consciously, and suddenly, you're more intentional in how you absorb everything life wants to offer. Look at you, singing love songs in the shower and serenading vegetables at the grocery store. You're so in love.

Finally, you know how it feels to be seen. To be held. To be considered. You're in love.

You feel cradled in this love and yet . . . sometimes trusting love is scary. You already fell in love, so why does it feel like you're still falling? You wonder, *What if I fall further than love can catch me?*

What do you do when you're safely in love but still afraid? You pause and think, *I don't have to lose myself to find love*. You remember that the Divine knows exactly where you are and where you will be. You let yourself go to where love is always found, which is exactly wherever you are.

Stop wasting good time worrying. Your fear won't stop a bad thing from coming, but it will stop you from enjoying the good thing that's already happening. Your fear will make you miss the moment. And your anxiety will make you rehearse scenes that will never be real. Prepare for the future by staying present in the love you have now. A love you manifested, and a love you were brave enough to return.

Friend, this love is yours. Your heart is ready, and so are you. When you're afraid, just whisper to yourself: *I'm scared, but I'm ready for this love.* And when you really need to, you can pull from this love. Remind yourself to draw courage from love; it'll help you dance when everyone's watching, speak a new language, and try new foods. And borrow the resilience from love that'll help you forgive when mistakes have been made and important dates are overlooked.

Let this love help you.

Let this love move you.

Let this love help you become you.

Daily Invitations

Invitation to affirm

I'm right where love can find me.
I'll take my time with this love.
I'm worthy of good love.
Write your own: ______________________________

Invitation to reflect

What do you appreciate most about this love story?
What's this love given you?
What space have you created for this love?
What are you giving to this love?
What does this love ask of you?

Invitation to commit

From today's soft landing:

The lesson I will take is ________________________.
The commitment I will make is ___________________.

SOFT LANDING #22

For the day you feel the warmth of friendship

Good friendship contains multitudes

Just when you thought you were going under, completely losing yourself to life's pressures, you felt their hand, perfectly timed and perfectly placed. In a world that can feel so hard, good friendship is the epitome of a soft landing.

You didn't know who was going to show up. After all, you planned the party at the last minute. But somehow, they all came. They made time for you. They came to see about you. You knew that your friends loved you, but today your heart is bursting with the realization that they'll do anything for you. How lucky could you be?! Your friends checked on your mom in the hospital, and they learned ASL so they could talk to your child. Thank all that is Good that you didn't escape this life without feeling the warmth of a friendship like this.

The goodness of friendship feels like a quilt, patched together with love, loyalty, respect, and vulnerability. On our best and worst days, friendship has been a trusted companion, an angel assigned to the specifics of our lives. It's completely imperfect, and somehow, still one of our best things.

Your friends don't wait till you've reached the mountaintop to celebrate but join in your joy along the journey. They check on your progress. They send texts that hype you up and quick prayers that keep you covered. In the moments, when the warmth of friendship feels like a hug, you remember that your friends are your chosen family. You honor the friends who plan group trips and parties, and the friends who brainstorm business ideas with you. The friends who are your patient advocates, and the ones who draft emails you're too afraid to write. The friends who show up to your grandmother's funeral, and the ones who organize meal trains.

If it's true that the best things in life are free, what do we make of the gift of friendship? We remark on its goodness and embrace it with the strength we've got. Friendship is a pure example of life's goodness that, if we're lucky, we can reflect back in the world.

I know that you can still remember being burned by that one friend, that hurt almost convinced you that you were better off doing life alone. But thank God for time, space, and forgiveness. The gratitude you feel in this moment, for these friends, reminds you that you couldn't have done this alone.

Friendship doesn't exist in your clean lines, but in the messy middle. The space you give each other when you're in two different seasons, and the honest conversations you have because some friendships are worth fighting for. The times you celebrate her win while you're experiencing your own loss, and when he supports you even when he doesn't understand your choices. Your best friendships aren't without accountability but they are marked with accountability that's wrapped in love. Friendship has helped you dream bigger dreams and communicate more honestly.

Good friendship has helped you ease into life.

No matter the season, you will always need friendship. As the seasons change, and so does your capacity, your soft landings will still be found within your community. We pray that days like today, when friendship's glow lights your way back home, you will always find a way to follow its path.

Daily Invitations

Invitation to affirm

I am worthy of good friendship.
I am a good friend.
I am thankful for my friends.
Friendship doesn't have to be perfect to be worthy of my embrace.
Write your own: ____________________

Invitation to reflect

How have you been a good friend this season?
What does good friendship look, feel, and sound like?
What are new ways you can support the friends in your life?

What does good friendship feel like?

What prompted your answer? (Be as specific as possible.)

Invitation to commit

From today's soft landing:

The lesson I will take is ______________________________.

The commitment I will make is ________________________.

SOFT LANDING #23

For the day you've been forgiven

Let the gift of grace change your life

You didn't think they were going to forgive you. Not this time. Not after what you did. Especially because, secretly, you knew better. It wasn't like this was a mistake; it was choice. And it wasn't the right one. In the aftermath of your bad choices, you've been begging grace to find you. Hoping mercy wouldn't forget your address.

"I forgive you."

Three words that invite evolution. Three words that offer accountability. Forgiveness unwraps new possibilities and second chances.

While considering this precious offering, it's tempting to fixate on your past mistakes and harmful behavior. But I urge you not to look at your past for too long—just look long enough so you can learn from it. Feelings of shame or even unhealthy pride may surface, too. Acknowledge their existence but be careful about giving them permission to make your choices. Don't let them stop you from opening your present. This forgiveness may not look like what society would call *just* or *fair*, but it's still yours. And it may feel like a bigger bag of grace than your arms can carry—but maybe that's a sign that you should put down your shame.

When we receive forgiveness, we receive a gift. An opportunity to be held by loving accountability and by someone's belief. You may not be ready for it, but that's the thing about gifts. A gift can arrive when we least expect it or haven't ask for it. With this gift of forgiveness, it's our job to say thank you and to really mean it. We show we mean it when we use it—and in this case we use forgiveness as a teacher and reminder. A reminder of how good it feels to be seen for more than our bad choices. And a teacher who says, stay prepared for the "next time."

With this forgiveness comes waves of joy and relief. Go ahead, examine and appreciate these feelings. Use them to expand your heart and to believe in yourself again. Even more, use them to believe in someone else. Let them help you remember, especially in your worst moments, that we can still find the best in each other.

You've not become so unlovable that forgiveness can't reach you. You're not so messed up that love can't find you.

Today is a good day and I hope you find the courage to enjoy it. Because sometimes, accepting that we've been forgiven is the most courageous thing we can do.

I hope you never forget just how good it feels to receive forgiveness. So that someday, when you need to, you can give it away, too.

Daily Invitations

Invitation to affirm

I am forgiven.

I don't have to be perfect to receive forgiveness.

I will embrace this slice of life's goodness.

Write your own: ________________________________

Invitation to reflect

What does it mean to sink into forgiveness?

Now that you've been forgiven, what is possible?

In a language of gratitude, how would you describe where you are now?

How do you want to move forward?

Invitation to commit

From today's soft landing:

The lesson I will take is __________________________.

The commitment I will make is ____________________.

SOFT LANDING #24

For the day you create something new

Good things come through you

Wow, wow, wow! Look at you! You bet on yourself. And you did it in a world that, for too long, has only told you what you didn't have, and that you weren't enough. In a society that equates credentials with self-esteem, you didn't wait for their approval to do what you knew you could. The world's tried everything to undermine your confidence, but *you believed you could, and you did.* You didn't wait until you had it all figured out before you placed your bet. You were patient, you were persistent, and you were relentless. All because you knew you were worth betting on. You *knew* you could do it. So is it really a bet if you already knew the outcome? I guess we'll never know.

You built something from a simple idea. You didn't run from the idea—you ran toward it. With tender hands, you nurtured it.

And when the time was right, you began to create something from it.

As days become nights, and you get further away from the immediate rush of creating, it's easy to overconcern yourself with what *they* will think. But before you go there, make sure you know what *you* think. I bet you think what you created is better than good. I bet you think it's incredible. And you should! As for us, the proverbial "they" who might enjoy your creation—maybe one day you'll give it over, but right now, what you created is for you. You don't have to be in a rush to share it, post it, or make money from it. You don't *ever* have to do those things. You can still create for creation's sake, honoring your purest expressions. You can do this because, as George A. Peters II likes to say, "Even if you weren't watching, I'd be doing this anyway."

You did it when we weren't watching. You did it because you wanted to.

When you're ready, you may look to refine your creation. And if you do, be sure to refine it in love, not harsh judgment. Don't erase the good along the way. Use your gentle hands as you take the next step, making sure not to confuse the aim for excellence with performative perfection. You've worked too hard to get distracted by such trivial things.

You know what we should do? Let's stop everything and take the next few seconds to celebrate what you did! I'm literally going to scream, woo-hoo! You can join me, or not. Either way, I'm still beaming for you.

In this moment, maybe you're feeling tempted to minimize your creation. I want to remind you that there's nothing small about betting on yourself. Every creation starts with a seed of an idea. And not every seed will take root. An idea's birth process is like that of a baby. There's a miraculous hidden germination and fertilization that uses the perfect mix of miracle and magic to bring things to life. The odds are stacked against that little seed. And more things must go right than wrong for the seed to become fully formed.

Your creation needed to be hidden in dark soil. But the darkness didn't scare you. You showed up, stood over your seed, and gave it water and nutrients. You gave it sunlight. You talked to it. You reminded it that, one day, it would be something great. When it sprouted above the soil, you got excited, not lazy. You were motivated by the progress, not fooled. You became even more disciplined and gave yourself the boundaries you needed to keep showing up. Before you knew it, that simple seed had turned into a plant, and that plant started to bear fruit! *You created something good.*

The fruit is more than the end product; it's a reminder of the journey. It's a reminder that you are capable, creative, and resourceful. Congratulations, friend! Please embrace the goodness of today. You created it.

Daily Invitations

Invitation to affirm

Good things can come from me.
I bring goodness into this world.

I am a vessel for good.

The journey was worth it.

Write your own: ______________________

Invitation to reflect

When was the first time you had this idea?

What habits supported your success?

Who's helped you along the way?

What boundaries were important? What self-talk worked?

How did you tend to yourself throughout this process? (Share any self-care practices, personal routines, and habits.)

What have you learned?

Invitation to commit

From today's soft landing:

The lesson I will take is ______________________.

The commitment I will make is ______________________.

SOFT LANDING #25

For the day it turns out better than expected

Let life surprise you

I bet you're still shaking your head in disbelief, wondering how it all worked out so well. I know that feeling, too. I've been there. Actually, I have a story I want to tell you.

At twenty-three, I was a naive Southern girl beginning a new life in New York City. Before my big move, I'd only taken nibbles out of the Big Apple; during one trip, I saw a massive subway rat, and on the other, I got lost on the A train in the Bronx. So even before getting the keys to my first apartment, I'd found the perfect subway map. My map was small enough to fit in my pocket but still big enough to read without giving too much tourist energy. I didn't leave the house without my map.

One morning, I hustled out of my apartment, iPod Shuffle in hand and my map safely tucked in my pocket. I walked the five blocks and two avenues to my subway stop and found my preferred spot on the platform. I was settling in for a brief wait when I saw a young woman, likely my age, confused and overwhelmed, desperately analyzing the map on the wall. I'd been that girl too many times before.

"She needs a map," I mumbled. And when I heard myself say it out loud, I knew I was about to give her my trusted map. As I approached her, I was still playing a game of internal tug of war. (Jovi, you've only lived here three months! You don't know where you're going! What about *your* safety? But it's the right thing to do!)

I put on my friendliest smile and said, "Hey, do you need help?" Sweaty and relieved, she smiled back.

"Yes, please."

I reached into my pocket and pulled out my perfect map.

"Here, take this map. It'll help you navigate in case you get lost." Shocked and grateful, she thanked me profusely. I shared a few more tips, and walked away, immediately convinced that now *I* was going to get lost. I kept telling myself I'd done the right thing, trying to believe that I was okay, and now she was, too.

Later that evening, I went to meet my coworkers at Caroline's for a comedy show. I was tempted not to go, especially because I wasn't as comfortable traveling without my map, but I went anyway. I made it without incident! When I arrived, my coworkers held my spot at the bar while I popped into the bathroom. I was washing my hands when I heard a woman say, "Oh my gosh, it's you." I looked up and there she was, the girl from the subway.

"I was just telling my friends about you! You were my angel this morning! I ended up getting an extra map today—you can have yours back. Thank you so much!"

The rest of our conversation was a blur (I think she was from

Minnesota?) as my utter shock and awe almost took me to my knees. What were the odds? Two strangers, in a city of millions, reuniting in a random bathroom in Times Square? Wow, wow.

But isn't that just like life—sometimes the thing you think could never happen happens. Or better yet, isn't that just like a God wink, when the exceedingly and abundantly above all you could ask for or think happens. These winks demand our attention, and, ideally, command our reverence.

Is this what you had today? A magic moment not to be missed but cherished. When we let it soak in, we let our awe bring tears and feel waves of reassurance that come from realizing we were never in control anyway. We remember we're a small piece of a larger design, but not so small that we'll ever be overlooked. When the superpower of the Divine chooses to mix with our natural steps, we experience a supernatural slice of life's goodness. These moments remind us that we should still believe in the magic of life. They remind us that miracles still happen—not just in movies but to us, too!

Sometimes, things work out so well that it's hard to believe it's real. It's tempting to think that we shouldn't tell anyone, that somehow, by sharing our miracle, it might lose its power. But miracles are meant to be witnessed, meant to be felt. You don't have to experience a miracle firsthand to be still transformed by its magic. When we share these miraculous moments, we see how their power can be exponential; one person who begins to believe in life's goodness can change the world. So yes, even when it's nerve-racking or scary, we should embrace life's miracles and share them with others. And while we know everything shouldn't be told to everyone, we can't let our discernment turn into silence.

We know how it feels when things don't work out. It's time we let ourselves feel the joy of when it does. On these days, when it feels like it's all too good to be true, remember that sometimes the really good is true. This sweet serendipity is yours. This sweet miracle is your life.

Don't forfeit your fairy tale; this happy ending has your name on it.

Daily Invitations

Invitation to affirm

Good things find me.
Miracles are made for me.
What's mine won't miss me.
I can take time to savor the good.
Write your own: ______________________________

Invitation to reflect

How are you feeling in this moment?
Gratitude extends when it's shared; who will you share gratitude with today?
What feels good about this moment?

Invitation to commit

From today's soft landing:

*The lesson I will take is*______________________________.
*The commitment I will make is*__________________________.

CONCLUSION

A Final Soft Landing

The work of being human is sacred. Make no mistake, honoring our humanity and the divine within is our highest calling. When we embody soft landing practices, we live fully into that assignment. We give ourselves space and grace to evolve. We are gentle with ourselves and allow ourselves slow down even when the world around us is speeding up.

I hope this book helps us stop negotiating ourselves out of our humanity. I hope it reminds you that we don't do life alone and that our healing is the true success story. As we walk this journey together, let's remember that we don't need to abandon ourselves to experience the soft landings we deserve.

When we lose our soft places to land, the world becomes brittle. Grace is eroded, and our larger culture loses empathy. I hope this book has been a call for collective restoration. We're not alone in our struggles, exhaustion, or self-doubt. The things that we think are personal failings are symptoms of a larger failing system that has categorically forgotten that we are precious human beings. This culture prizes production over presence, and it will pull everything it can out of us if we don't radically push back and reset the terms of our engagement. Our collective practice of soft landings will help us protect ourselves by remembering that compassion isn't something nice-to-have; it is a fundamental must-have. We don't need to prove we deserve to land more softly when we were already born worthy.

Around the world, in various countries, we see how an inequitable capitalist and partriarchal society hinges upon our fear: fear of being last, of being without, and of being powerless. At the time I'm writing this book, the United States government, under the administration of a demented leader parading as a president, is leaning heavily into this fear. We're witnessing an active reversion to the worst of our history: new age Jim Crow laws, unlawful raids in Black and Brown communities, policy rollbacks protecting the most vulnerable, and a calculated campaign to erase the accurate storytelling of the country's history, just to start. Where we would normally want to appreciate the good, we feel ourselves overwhelmed, swept away by a rip current of negativity. The impact of this onslaught of evil on our minds is undeniably heavy and, in many ways, unavoidable, and yet, it reminds me how important it is for us now, more than ever, to appreciate life's goodness. This is a bold choice in the face of fear.

This attack is planned and diabolically schemed by the historically powerful—*but* it's not the end of our story. When we remember that there has always been good amid our flawed and evil actions, we can continue our part in writing a story that is still unfolding. If we can give ourselves a soft landing, we can spread it. Evil is betting on our fatigue, apathy, and overwhelm, but I'm betting on our ability to *still* appreciate and share life's goodness. The goodness that makes us more responsible, loving, and committed citizens. The kind that reminds us we are responsible for each other and the earth we've been gifted.

So much of our self-doubt is seeded from outsized structural inequities. The giants attacking our worthiness are systemic in nature and institutional in statute. To sustain our fight we can collectively be hard on the systems and soft on ourselves. This phrase is how we remember to link arms, encourage each other, and have each other's backs. It reminds us that we shouldn't push for macro change alone, but in community or partnership. It's why we win when we phone bank legislators together and agree to mentor one another. It's why our community organizations exist and why volunteering in packs is important. It's how we'll have the energy for the long haul. Together we find new resolve, inspiration, and courage. If you have to tap out, I'm there to tap in. We don't quit, we rotate. When together, we're hard on the systems, we help each remain soft—we help each other remember the very precious humanity we're fighting for.

There will be days when we'll still be too hard on ourselves, entertaining harmful expectations or capitulating to requests that cross our boundaries. And when we do, we will remember to pick up grace, not judgment. We will keep honoring ourselves because we love ourselves. The soft landing practices we explore in this book are five of many that can usher us into a more loving relationship with ourselves and others. We can keep learning and exploring.

I wrote this book while I still had time to love myself better.

You picked up this book because the title reached your tender, unseen places. It spoke to the suppressed needs you were convinced to believe didn't matter. But now, hopefully, you remember that they do matter and always have. Trust the work that's led to this clarity. Your refined intuition costs you something. Unlike the paradox of progress you were caught in before, you're no longer running further from yourself. You're returning home to a softer place.

When you forget that you deserve to land softly, get still, get quiet, and listen to your guides. Don't worry if your soft landings feel countercultural. Remember the words of Maya Angelou and Toni Morrison. Sit with Thích Nhạt Hanh and Jesus the carpenter. Remember how they taught us that it was okay to steal away from the world so you can keep what is yours. Don't worry about rushing to perform publicly what's unfolding privately. Intentionally live into your new soft landings until they become sacred, unconscious acts of love. And before you know it, your heart will once again become your home.

Thank you for being here. It was wonderful to spend time with you. I hope you have landed as softly as I have.

With love,
Jovian

Acknowledgments

It seems antithetical, but what I've learned is that to soar high, you have to be anchored below. My anchors are deep and strong, characterized by my abiding family, resolute friends, insightful colleagues, and abundant community members. They flank me like angels on assignment.

I alone could never have written this book, but infused with their encouragement, I could write twenty. It's through blurry, tear-filled eyes that I say thank you.

To everyone who's seen me, the real me, the Jovi who's always known she was meant to encourage the human spirit, thank you. You wouldn't let me forget myself. Thank you for holding up the mirror so I wouldn't have to question who I was. Though I don't have the capacity to name all of you, please know that even if you don't see your name, I'm talking to you. You have made a difference in my journey.

George, you've helped me birth two children. First Jorgie, and now my book baby. In both experiences, you prayed over me, with me, and for me. You concerned your heart for my well-being and purpose, and those concerns have turned into your strategic support, deliberate dedication, and enveloping encouragement. Thank you for prioritizing your relationship with God so you could love me even better. Your leadership and covering are evidence of God's promise for me. I knew I could love you when you inspired me to start writing in 2008. I knew I would love you when you told me to never stop. Your commitment to the intentional, not reckless, abandon with which you dream is the innocence that defines the very best childhoods and now our marriage. Thank you for helping me live into my dreams. I love you so, so much. Dreammates forever.

Jorgie, thank you for choosing me as your mother. And for getting on that water slide down from heaven and entering this complicated world. You're the best personal and professional development I could ever ask for, ha! Thank you for praying for me! For loving me! For trusting me! You are intrepid. Insightful. Hilarious. Grounded. And wise beyond your years. I wrote this book for you, my dear. Give this to others so they know how to love you well.

To my very first soft landing: Mama, Daddy, Trey, and Roman. I love you so very much. What we have as a family is anointed, and it's a bond that will never be broken. "Just having you there," just like we sang at my wedding, has made all the difference. I am who I am because you've loved me first. You've seen me first. Until George came along, you've been my biggest champions, without exception. Thanks for pulling my skirt when I needed it and thanks for making me laugh at myself. "Hello, Heidi!" And at the same time, thank you for making sure that I took myself very seriously.

Mama and Daddy, you are the unequivocal blueprint. Your imperfectly persistent and committed love for each other and our family is the dream for my life. Thank you for being the worthy standard that has overcome the world's distorted notion of love. Trey and Roman: You've given me direction on how to bet on myself. How to study my craft and have fun doing it. Thank you for being womb-mates, strategic partners, and still the best playmates. I'll love you forever!

Sister Siblings: Janelle. Your wisdom, honesty, authenticity, and courage have been such a light to me. I am braver, kinder, and more adventurous and kind because of our sisterhood. Thank you for teaching me! Encouraging me! And hyping me up!!! Nange: Thank you for being an example of creativity and dedication! Steph: Your joy, love, and caring spirit is a GIFT. Thank you for watching Jorgie so I could write. ☺

Mama Jean, to have your prayers is to have the world. Thank you for always telling me stories that remind me where I come from. Mama Gladys, thank you for writing with me. Aunt Ruth, thank you for publishing your book before mine and giving me something to aspire to! To all of my aunts and uncles, great-aunts and -uncles, cousins, and the like—I am proud to call you my family!

To my in-loves: Thank you for encouraging me and offering me support! Thank you for the gift of George.

Brittany and Gia: What can I say? We have prayed this thing through, haven't we? Wow. Look what God has done. Thank you, thank you.

Winning Walk Wednesday Crew: IJ, Mya, Angel. Every Wednesday, we've walked this thing out. Every mile of our friendship has been a soft landing. I love you!

The Cabinet: Amber, IJ, Lily, and Becca. I love y'all so much. We do life together, forever! You are my soft place to land, always.

AS Crew: It was during a prayer at one NYC holiday dinner that I said, "In a city that can be so hard, we have been each others' soft place to land." The title was solidified with our truth. The years of brunches, road trips, group chats, and late nights gave this book a genuine heartbeat.

Ebonites: Camille, Lauren, Morgan, Adrienne, and Khali—Wow, our mothers are an example of what it means to love each other for decades, and I know that we will, too. Thank you for the encouragement, prayer, and advocacy. Thank you Ebonite Mamas/Aunties!

Early readers: Morgan, Lily, Callan, George, Jen. You've been extraordinary truth tellers. Thank you for your time, energy, and honesty. Morgan, you really helped me push this thing to the next level. Thank you for being my soft landing and for picking up the phone time and time again.

Natalie and Marquita, our walks have been a balm. Our conversations, spiritual nourishment. I'm forever grateful for how we show up for each other, and more importantly, how much we show up for God's call. I'm so honored that you share your heart with me. I'll never take it for granted.

Sophie and Charity—thank you for helping me discover the early fuel for my journey. Carrie and Jen—your friendship, example, and encouragement mean the world. Luvvie—you have midwifed my book along with so many others. Your heart is so generous. I love you! Thank you for establishing the Book Academy family—an invaluable community and resource. TBA fam, I appreciate you! Nyla, you've been with me from the beginning. I love you and thank you. God hears our prayers!

Polaris family: To all of my co-facilitators, thank you for being excellent mirrors and containers for my reflection and growth. To Amanda and Joy, you're two of the greatest co-facilitators I've ever known, and our time together has changed my life. Thank you so very much for being extraordinary colleagues and now dear friends.

To my Delta Sigma Theta Sorority, Incorporated Sorors: Thank you linesisters, specs, big sisters, and sorors for the sisterhood and love. There is no other way! To the Fab 5: Always sisters, always friends!!! Thank you for the calls, prayers, and constant encouragement.

Tiffany and Carla, thank you for being my big sisters, mentors, and advocates. I love you and I am forever grateful!

Wondaland fam: Thanks for the strategic and creative advice. From agent meetings to strategy sessions—you've continually held me down!

Carolina's Finest and The Whole: Thank you for the years of friendship and love.

To every person who gave an encouraging word, whether through an in-person exchange or voice note, phone call, email, or text, THANK YOU! To everyone who replied to my requests for stories or reflections, thank you!!! Your perspective was invaluable.

To my past and current (shout-out to Pastor Churn) leadership at Old Storm Branch Baptist Church, Zion Baptist Church, Mt. Zion Baptist Church, Greater Allen A.M.E. Cathedral, and First

Corinthian Baptist Church, thank you for edifying my faith and giving me a chance to lead.

My soft landings team, thank you, thank you! I couldn't have done this without you.

Cathy Fyock, my first book coach. Thank you for helping me ritualize my writing experiences. You taught me to write with a plan. Kari, you believed in me on day one. That laugh of yours confirmed what my heart knew; you have a joy that's kinetic and a heart for my work that will keep us grounded and committed. Thank you for truly seeing me and walking this path with me. It's UP!!! Nina, thank you for understanding the heart behind my words and giving them space to beat. You refined ugly first drafts and gave me insightful feedback that helped me to return home to myself even stronger, and with a clearer vision. You've been such an extraordinary partner in this process.

Thanks to Meg and the entire Penguin team for their efforts to bring more soft landings into this world.

I wrote this book in lots of places. Sometimes in the car after a tough conversation. Other times staring in the mirror via voice note.

Most often, it was in coffee shops where I could daydream, ear hustle, and experience life with earnest strangers. To the places that let me do that most honestly, Humblebee, Sotta, and Basecamp, thank you. Shout-out to Brian, Victoria, and Tangy at Humblebee. You passed me tissues and gave me extra juice. I wasn't your average customer, and you didn't treat me as such. Thank you so much.

To everyone who believes in the power of soft landings, thank you for joining me. Stay close, I get the feeling we're just getting started.